Writing Romance

The Top 100 Best Strategies For Writing Romance Stories

By Alessandra Bancroft
Copyright © 2015

Table of Contents

Introduction 3
Chapter 1: Romance Preparations 5
Chapter 2: Story Basics 19
Chapter 3: Romance Your Characters 31
Chapter 4: Romantic Story Goals 46
Chapter 5: Romantic Outlines 50
Chapter 6: Romance Writing - Tips and Strategies 56
Chapter 7: Romantic Storylines 61
Chapter 8: The Grand Finale 65
Conclusion 67
My Other Books and Audio Books 68

Introduction

I want to thank you and congratulate you for downloading the book, "Writing Romance: The Top 100 Best Strategies For Writing Romance Stories."

Romance is an exciting and emotion-invoking genre of fiction that focuses on the relationship between two characters, traditionally a man and a woman. Stories about romance have been around as far back as the 18th century, with Jane Austen ranking as one of the most notable authors. Originally popular in the United Kingdom, romance stories became a trend in the United States in the 1970's starting with *The Flame and the Flower*, the first published romance novel of its kind. Today, romance is the most popular genre of fiction in North America. 55% of all paperback books sold in the U.S. in 2004 fell under romance. There are many subgenres of romance, including historical, paranormal, fantasy and sci-fi. In the past few years, erotica has also seen an increase in popularity.

Since romance is a dominating genre across the market, many authors have found it to be one of the best genres to write. Annually, the total sales for romance books average to be about $1.08 billion dollars, making it a very lucrative writing opportunity. As technology and media have been on the rise, romance now accounts for 39% of e-books from companies such as Amazon and Barnes and Noble, exceeding mass-market paperback format by 7% and trade paperback by 21%.

Fiction writing is generally very creative and has little room for rules but romance writing brings together a few guidelines to help you ensure that your story is hitting the right triggers for your target audience. A typical romance story includes **five key elements**: a heroine, a seductive hero, emotional conflict, and an engaging plot, all wrapped up with a happy, satisfying ending. Many authors disagree on other elements of romance, such as when the protagonists need to meet or whether or not the ending must be happy. While there is no proven formula for writing a romance story, writing in this genre is generally flexible, as long as one stays true to the five key elements.

According to The Romance Writers of America, "the main plot of a romance novel must revolve around two people as they develop romantic love for each other and work to build a relationship." The conflict and suspense must directly tie into the romantic theme of the story. The definition also requires a romance story to have an "emotionally satisfying and optimistic ending."

Romance writing can be your ticket to success, as long as you know what you're doing. This book contains proven steps and strategies on how to expand upon the five key elements of romance writing to craft a story that readers are looking for. Within the pages of this book, you will discover how to successfully write a solid, well-structured romance story that may very well lead to a wealthy outcome.

First, you will explore all the best ways to prepare yourself for romance writing, including basic writing advice and tips that are specific to the romance genre. You will then discover everything you will need to get a handle on the basics of your story. Following that, you will learn how to develop strong and compelling characters to supplement your storyline. You will also discover practical story ideas, tips, and strategies that will help you write a strong romance, different ways to outline and structure your story and how to give your characters exciting and engaging story goals that will have your readers dying to know the outcome.

Romance is a huge genre; every day you can find new romance novels and eBooks released to slake the thirst of an avid romance-devouring audience. The competition is lively, but if you can master the ropes of writing a romance novel, employing all the characteristics your audience desires, and contributing to the genre with your unique voice, you have a chance of breaking into the world of success. So, what are you waiting for? Discover what you need to get started right here, then go out and get your name up there in the lights of the romance firmament!

Chapter 1: Romance Preparations

You've finally got a great idea and you're feeling inspired to start writing your book. You sit down at your computer, open up a blank document and just start typing away as fast as you can, right? Think again. While many prospective authors imagine it is plausible to just do that, there is actually one very important step you should take if you want to be successful in writing romance. That step is **preparation**. Preparation is an important part of accomplishing anything, not just writing. Authors are no different from athletes who prepare for their wins or businesspeople who prepare oral presentations. Authors prepare themselves to write their next best-seller. Preparation helps you anticipate each part of your story and frees your creativity to develop entrancing ideas. Proper preparation will reduce any anxiety you have about your writing venture.

As an author, I believe that preparation is the most vital part of writing a book. I also believe that everybody has their own personal way of preparing. Writing is a creative activity in itself. I know several authors who each have their own unique preparation routines. It all depends on you and your personal preferences. In this chapter, I will discuss some of the best ways to prepare yourself for the task of writing, but it's up to you to pick out what suits you best.

So, exactly how *does* one prepare to write a great romance novel?

How to Identify a Romance

A successful romance writer must know the difference between an actual romance novel and a novel that happens to contain a love story. Get this distinction clear in your mind before you engage your writing gears. It can be difficult to discern between the two, because both revolve around characters who fall in love. The key difference is that in a romance the love story is essential.

Think of it this way: if you removed the element of romantic relationship from your story, what would be left? If you delete it and there is little to no story remaining, then you've got yourself a romance novel. If you delete the romantic element and your story still is intact. you may be writing in an entirely different genre.

For example, let's say you're writing a story about a man whose mental condition deteriorates due to traumatic events that include a break-up with his girlfriend. If you omit the breakup between the man and his girlfriend you've still got a story, one that centers on the regression of the man's mental state.

Read Fiction

All romance writers should be widely-read across the literature spectrum. Since romances may appear within the guise another fiction subgenre, your preparation should include choosing the type of fiction you plan to use as the base for your romance. In addition to general fiction, here are a few types of fiction that lend themselves well to romance writing:

- Historical – Set in a specific historical era.

- Epistolary – Structure consists of a series of letters between characters

- Mystery – Solve a crime or uncover a secret

- Tragedy – The story ends badly for the main characters; for a romance, think Romeo and Juliet

- Fantasy – Mystical or imaginary creatures, often in an imagined setting

You can read all you want *about* the various types of fiction, but to truly absorb what makes them distinctive, I recommend reading several novels from your chosen fiction sub-category. The more familiar you become with a given type of fiction, the better you will understand how you can capitalize on that subgenre's characteristics when you write your romance.

If you familiarize yourself with the types of fiction that are out there, you will more easily identify your story's place within the fiction market, you will better understand the competition, and you will be well-prepared to write a novel that stands out from all the rest.

Understanding your particular subgenre is a strong unifying force. It will help you write in a consistent voice throughout the book. It will also save you much time, agony, and rewriting effort in the future. We will discuss subgenres in greater detail in the next chapter, but for now it is only important to be aware that they exist and will influence your romance writing going forward.

Write From Your Life

My best advice is to write the story you have inside you. Many writers make the mistake of writing a romance just because they've heard it will sell easily. However, if your heart is not in the story, your readers will know it and will dismiss you from the start. Don't write just to fit your story into a specific niche; if you can't see where your story belongs, write it first, and then think about which type of story it most closely matches.

A book that grows out of your personal experiences will naturally tend to sound realistic, largely because it is based upon things that actually happened…to you. This kind of a book will be much easier to write and will depend more heavily upon your personal knowledge and expertise than upon imagination and mere conjecture.

It's always best to write from your own life experiences. I have one friend who was able to write a book about a fast food restaurant, because she worked in the industry for years. Another friend based a highly compelling romance novel on one of her own relationships.

Research

While it is important to write what you know, you will probably run into places where you just haven't experienced something your characters are living through. For example, if your main character is a doctor, she will need to execute any number of tasks you know nothing about. If you try to bluff your way through by using vague descriptions, your readers will likely feel cheated. After all, one of the reasons people pick up your book in the first place is to be able to experience what it is like to be – in this instance – a doctor. In order to immerse themselves in the scene, they require the very thing you are unable to give – vivid details.

The solution is to fill in your knowledge gaps with research. Yes, research is hard work and takes time away from actual writing. However, you want your book to shine, don't you? Then dig in; burn up Google with those internet searches (triple checking facts for accuracy). Make the reference librarian your new pal – yes, darken the door of your local library for reference materials, autobiographies, and to find other fiction books with similar focus to your own (just be careful to avoid plagiarism). You can also use case law, case studies, textbooks, or other how-to books to put yourself in a character's shoes. In short, revel in the joy of learning everything you can about your subject. Then, step out and make friends with people who work in the field you are writing about.

The next best alternative to writing from personal experience is to interview those who have the experience you need. Don't be afraid to approach others and ask for an interview. Nine times out of ten a person will be happy to share their knowledge, especially if they know they are helping you write a book. Loyal professionals are usually eager to help you "get it right" when depicting their profession.

Don't forget to thank these helpers, both verbally and in writing, for their assistance. It never hurts to show your gratitude later by providing a signed copy of the finished product after it is published.

In addition to research and directly interviewing subject matter experts, I also recommend visiting the setting of any scenes you are researching. In our medical example, a visit to a surgical theatre will offer up hundreds of vivid details your readers need in order to immerse themselves in an operating scene. If you are able to hang out in a hospital for a day, just keeping your ears open may net some key phrases, attitudes, and jargon that can add realism and depth to your characters, descriptions and dialogue. After you have soaked up the atmosphere of the place you will find it much easier to describe for your readers.

Prepare For Criticism

As popular as romance is, it is often accompanied by lots of criticism. Many people believe that all romance stories are essentially the same and authors just rearrange the details for their next story. Some critics theorize that romance novels victimize women by presenting them as helpless and emotionally weak. Others believe that romance stories cause women to idealize men. Between being weak and idealizing men some folks think this encourages the notion that women need a man to take of them.

Some readers will criticize your ideas or your writing style. Criticism hurts. Even the most constructive criticism can be painful. It can be very discouraging to have your "baby" disparaged by a crass, insensitive public. Over time, however, you will learn to distinguish constructive criticism from heartless, soul-crushing bashing. I encourage you to keep yourself open to constructive criticism, even when it is painful. Reject whatever attacks you as a person and instead focus on nuggets of Truth that will help you hone your writing skills.

The Meaning of Success

How does one define a writer? There are probably as many definitions as there are writers. Many would argue that a successful writer has a special talent or skill. Others would define a successful writer as one who has obtained special training or reached a certain level of notoriety. A writer may also be someone with connections in the publishing industry.

Here is my personal definition: I believe a successful writer is a person with a talent for writing, who is also willing to devote time to perfecting their craft. The craft can be perfected through trial and error, by taking classes, or through self-education (by reading books like this one, for example). A successful writer is a person who can learn from the critiques of others and push himself to grow as a writer. A successful writer writes regularly, even when it's not relative to his or her current work. A successful writer writes and rewrites, edits and re-edits. A successful writer is passionate about getting across a message.

Of course, it helps to have publishing connections. You can start building those relationships by attending writing events and seminars, all of which can help you improve your craft.

You may think a successful writer is one who ultimately gets published and makes enough money to retire at a young age. Although that level of success can be extremely difficult to achieve, it is not impossible. Most people know that J.K. Rowling, author of the Harry Potter series, started out as a struggling single mom. Today she is the well-known author of multiple books, many of which have since been turned into highly popular movies.

While connections in the writing world can definitely help you get ahead, it is essential to know what publishers and readers are looking for. There is nothing wrong with contacting publishers directly, to learn what they are interested in publishing. Check out bestseller lists and look for common subjects and themes. Monitor news outlets and keep abreast of trending topics of interest. All of these can help you frame your story as an audience magnet.

Maybe you are not interesting in being published. If you just want to write for yourself, you are still a writer; your definition of success is just narrowed down to an audience of one.

I highly recommend taking some time to define your own success. Writing about it will help make it solid in your mind as you continue your literary quest.

Define Your Writing Goal

Once you have defined what it takes to be a successful writer, you should define your writing goal. Setting goals as a writer is a little more complex than setting goals for other achievements, such as dieting or fitness. Why? As a writer, you actually have *two* goals: your own personal goal and the goal of providing your audience with a satisfying experience.

Your personal writing goal is a variable. You might make it a long-term goal to write a novel or a short story or a series of stories. Your long-term goal could even be to become a published author. Your short-term goals should provide stepping-stones to your long-term goals and help you, slowly but surely, achieve ultimate success. For example, if you want to become a published author, then your short-term goal should include writing your first novel. However, to write your first novel, you will need an additional set of even shorter-term goals that include the completion of each chapter. To achieve those goals, you will probably need to set daily writing objectives. Many authors set a specific word count quota in order to help them stay on track and finish within a desired timeframe.

No matter what your writing goal may be, it is important to remember your ultimate objective. Every author must work toward this goal to be successful (by their definition). Part of that success means you must know how to gain popularity with your target audience; you must provide your readers with an **emotional experience.** To achieve this, you must first recognize why people want to pick up a book in the first place.

Most people who enjoy reading say they see it as an escape from their own reality. Many readers like to put themselves in a different world so that they can experience emotions they otherwise wouldn't encounter in everyday life. They like to feel moved, touched and inspired. They like to feel danger, fear, and suspense. They like to be moved to feel happiness and sadness.

This is why it is so important to learn multiple techniques and elements of romance writing. If your book is boring and the pace drags, your readers will not be able to immerse themselves in the story and will more than likely put your book down after the first few pages. If your book is filled with conflict and emotion, your readers will get what they're looking for. You will learn more about how to successfully provide your readers with an emotional experience as we progress through this book but for now, take out a piece of paper, or your journal, and write down your two writing goals. For your fixed goal, you can simply state that you will provide your readers with an emotional experience. You can go back and make it more specific as you discover just what that takes.

Know Your Writing Level

The next step is to figure out what level you are on as a writer. I say this because it helps you figure out where you currently are compared to where you want to be. When figuring out what level you are on, you must be completely honest with yourself, otherwise you will never advance. Writing levels generally begin with the novice and progress to the inexperienced writer, then the experienced writer, and culminate in the expert.

A **novice** writer is typically just starting out. That's okay. Everybody has to start somewhere. A novice writer usually knows that he or she wants to write something and has the ambition to take them there, but may not understand what is necessary to really pack a punch with an audience or how to actually put a book together. An **inexperienced** writer is typically someone who has exercised their writing talent before and may know how to put a book together, but they still need to improve their skills and sharpen their craft. An **experienced** writer is dedicated to writing and probably attends classes or networking events; this writer may have self-published a few times. An **expert** writer is one who has written several works, is familiar with the craft and the ins and outs of publishing, has connections among other writers and publishers, and may have been published by a major publishing house.

Ask yourself where you think you stand on the writing spectrum and make a note of it. Part of your writing goal can be to move up a level until you've become an expert. Always remember that no matter what level you're on, there is always room for improvement; writing is a lifelong growth process.

Get Organized

As a writer, organization should be on the top of your priority list for two reasons. First, your workspace must be easy to navigate; you must know where to find things without wasting precious writing time hunting around. Secondly, people tend to work most efficiently and creatively in an uncluttered environment. A clean and neat working area can actually make you feel good about yourself, which only feeds productivity and creativity. I'm reminded of a friend who was visited in his office by a well-dressed and neatly coiffed woman. The lady took one look at his desk, piled high with papers and research books, sniffed slightly, and stated, "You know; a cluttered desk is a sign of a cluttered mind." My friend thought for a moment, looked up at the woman, and asked, "Then, what does an empty desk signify?"

Personally, I'm way too distracted by a mess; any type of clutter pulls my focus away from my work. Consequently, here are my personal workspace organizational tips:

- Keep a towel or duster nearby and dust your work area once a day. This helps keep your workspace clean and avoids upsetting your allergies, if you have any.

- Keep wires (such as your laptop charger, printer cord, and associated USB cables) together and organized, using twist ties.

- Put your pens, pencils, and scissors together in a pen holder; a spare coffee mug works great for this purpose.

- Keep your important papers together in a paper tray or a file rack.

- Avoid eating or drinking in your workspace, but if you do, clean up the area immediately afterwards.

Assuming that you're using a computer to write your book, it is also important to stay digitally organized. I know from personal experience that when you start to write a book on your computer, one document can quickly turn into many. I often use individual documents to track characters, chapter notes, a timeline of events, synopses, and outlines. It is easy to lose track of those files within your hard drive, especially if you have a lot of stuff on your system.

Although you may not immediately identify these next items as aspects of writing, you do need to organize your time, your energy, and your money. If you are working under a deadline, you automatically understand the importance of managing your time. Even if you don't have an externally imposed deadline, I recommend setting a rough target date for completion of your next writing project, then scheduling your work to meet that objective.

Parkinson's Law states that work expands to fill the amount of time allotted to it. If you don't set a deadline, guess what? Your writing project may well take until doomsday to complete! You will work a lot more efficiently if you divide the work up into manageable chunks, then shoot to complete each chunk in a reasonable amount of time.

Giving yourself a "due date" will stimulate you to write on a regular basis. Writing a book does take time, but if you manage it correctly, it's not as bad as it may seem. You can manage your time several ways, but the most popular time management technique for writing is to set a daily writing quota for yourself, in terms of number of words. There are two possible ways to set both a writing quota and a deadline. The first way is to decide how much you want to write each day and divide the total size of your book, in number of words, by the by that amount. This will give you the number of days it will take to complete your first draft. You can map this on a calendar to determine your projected completion date. The other method is to decide when you want to finish your first draft, then work backwards from that date, calculating how many writing days you have before the deadline. Divide the total estimate for the book's word count by the number of days you plan to work, and you will know how many words you will need to write each day in order to meet your deadline.

Managing your time also includes planning breaks. Our bodies were not designed to sit still for hours on end. Recent studies have shown that as little as three hours of inactivity can be enough to affect our bodies negatively. Eyestrain is also possible in this line of work. It is important to take the eyes off the computer at least a couple times an hour, to look around you. When you can, take a few minutes outside; your eyes need to relax by looking into the distance for a change, and your whole being will benefit from a little intake of fresh air and natural sunlight.

We also need to periodically give our minds a break from thinking about the current writing project. Unfortunately, the mind does not have an "off" switch; the best way to give your mind a break is to divert it with something else that requires your attention. Any physical activity that requires a little attention will serve as a healthy break for both mind and body. I sometimes go outside to play with the dog or pull weeds in the garden. If I can't get outside, even a little light housecleaning is enough to get me moving and distracted from the computer for a few minutes.

The final organizational issue involves managing your money. You may not think about your writing costing any money and for the most part, you are correct. But you will likely incur a few expenses, if only for printer paper and ink for occasional printouts, and the cost of internet access, for conducting research and communication with potential publishers. In addition, you may choose to invest in books that will help you as a writer; you may enroll in personal improvement classes, or pay for professional editing. Many writing seminars and conventions also cost money to attend. It is wise to allocate at least a small amount in your budget for writing expenses.

Choose a Writing Space

Every author needs a writing space, the place where you do the majority of your work. The most popular spots are at a desk in your home (preferably in a home office) or at a coffee shop, library, or another public venue. Some people can't focus when working in a public place like a coffee shop, but others thrive there. I've tried working on my laptop outside on several occasions but I've found it difficult when I don't have shelter from the sun. My personal preference is to sit at my desk and work. You might find comfort by working from your couch. Whatever you choose, set up your work in a comfortable location where you can work most productively.

Eliminate Distractions

As a writer, I must admit my top excuse for slacking off is any of the multiple distractions that come my way. Working on a computer can be the worst, because email, social media, music, and other attractive, activities are all too accessible. Even if you manage to avoid computer-based distractions, you can still access everything from your phone, which you probably keep close by. Then there are always the household distractions, your spouse, kids, or pets whose interruptions are almost irresistible. A quick and easy fix for this is to close the door to your office and hang up a do not disturb sign. I've tried writing outdoors before, but I've found that to be even more distracting than my children. I've endured everything from sunlight glaring on my screen, to babies crying in the neighborhood, to visits from stray dogs.

As for digital distractions, I've found it helpful to work in full-screen mode. This way, my eyes are less likely to wander off to whatever lies behind what I'm writing. I've also made it a point to mute my phone until I'm done writing. For audible distractions, I have discovered that earbuds will block out an incredible amount of noise, even without playing music through them.

Set the Mood

I personally find it helpful to set the mood before I begin a writing session. Depending on what kind of story I'm writing, I'll do different things. I've found that aromatherapy is a great strategy for relaxing and getting into a positive state of mind. It is also great for trying to get into a sensual state of mind when writing ro. You can practice aromatherapy right in your own workspace by getting a small oil diffuser and some different oils to experiment with. My favorite way to fill a room with pleasant smelling aromas is with an oil diffuser. Some great smelling essential oils I recommend are:

- Lavender – known for its relaxing qualities, it also smells heavenly

- Eucalyptus – strong, earthy, but pleasantly scented, it is thought to clear the mind

- Marjoram Leaves

- Peppermint

- Chamomile

- Cloves
- Cinnamon Bark
- Sage
- Rosemary
- Cardamom
- Verbena

In other situations, I find it helpful to play music in the background while I'm writing. The type of music I listen to usually depends on the genre I'm writing, but I try to stick to instrumental tracks; tracks with lyrics tend to distract me. If I'm writing a sad or depressing scene I like to listen to classical music, such as Beethoven or Mendelssohn. If I'm writing a thrilling, action scene I'll go onto Spotify and look up soundtracks from my favorite movies to get me in the mood. Spotify also has some great playlists with romantic music. Just search for the term "romantic" in the search bar and go under playlists. You can also look up some Pandora.com instrumental tracks that are relaxing in general and let them play in the background as another option.

Practice Self-Discipline

Writing a book will take lots of self-discipline. I've written and published several books and have had people come up to me and say, "Wow, I could never do that!" It's not easy and sometimes it is even tempting to give up. I've gone through phases where I will trudge right through a book and others where I'll start a book, only to drop it for a couple months. A disciplined life is essential if you hope to finish your book. For some people, self-discipline comes easily, but for those of you struggle to be disciplined, here are some tips to help you reinforce yourself:

1. Be aware of what happens when you *don't* write anything. A big self-discipline killer is when you say thing like, "I'll do it when I feel like it." Well, what if you *don't* feel like it for the next couple of days? Let's say you have made it a goal to write one chapter of your book each day, but one morning you wake up and just don't feel like writing at all. Even a day or two without keeping your commitment to yourself will set you back to the point that it will be difficult to completely catch up. It is much better to meet your goals, even if it hurts. You will feel much better afterwards.

2. Stop making excuses. When it comes to writing a book, there are no excuses. Writer's block is not an excuse either. When you say something like, "I'm too tired to write today" or "I can't think of any good ideas," you're only setting yourself back. Write something every day, even if it's

just a little bit of free-writing. Never let an excuse take over your chosen life.

3. Get yourself an accountability partner. Find somebody who will hold you responsible for accomplishing the things you have committed to. This can be a huge help. My suggestion is to enlist the help of somebody who already serves as your mentor or role model; it will be harder to let down a person you respect and want to emulate than your best friend or your spouse. Sometimes best friends will let you off the hook far too easily. You want to find somebody who can be trusted to hold your feet to the fire when necessary.

Generate Self-Motivation

Along with self-discipline, you're going to need some self-motivation to get the job done. Procrastination is an obstacle that often prevents people from actually writing an entire book, so you'll need become an anti-procrastinator before you even sit down in front of your computer.

One powerful technique many authors use is to ask "why." Why do you want to write a romance story? Popular answers include being able to see your name on the cover or so that you can entertain people. Some people simply have a story that they need to get out. Go ahead and figure out your why. I think it is helpful to write this down and keep it visible in your workspace, to consistently motivate yourself to keep going.

Another motivational technique is to promise yourself a reward at the end. Writing a book is a big task, so if you have a big reward waiting for you afterwards, you're going to be much more likely to finish. I can't tell you what your reward will be–that's up to you to choose–but make it something you really, *really* want. You may choose a material object such as a new TV or video game system, others choose a short vacation, but for some people, just seeing the book in print is reward enough.

Finally, I have found that exercising can be motivational as well. Exercising allows your body to feel alive, so you'll have an overall "feel-good" sensation to carry into your writing. I think the better you feel physically, the better you'll be able to perform your writing. When I work out, I start to feel inspired to tackle other major accomplishments. Exercising is also a useful way to spend your "break" time. You already spend enough time sedentarily before your computer; break it up by moving your body, and you may be pleasantly surprised with some fresh ideas when you return to your writing.

Eat Before Writing

One of the most important things you can do to get ready for writing is to eat beforehand! Eating a meal can give you a burst of mental energy, which you can then pour out into your book. If you try to write on an empty stomach, you may find it harder to concentrate; you might even do something crazy, like name a character after food! The best types of foods to eat before writing are those that will stimulate your brain. Let's look at a few examples:

1. Fruits and Vegetables – These foods are full of antioxidants that are good for fueling your creativity. Experts believe blueberries are the most effective. Whip up some blueberry pancakes, a blueberry smoothie or simply just snack on some blueberries straight up.

2. Omega-3 Fatty Acids – This substance is known to boost the functioning of your brain, which you're definitely going to need as a writer. You can provide your body with omega-3 fatty acids through fish such as salmon or mackerel, or through flax seed. To avoid eating actual fish, you can always supplement your healthy diet with fish oil capsules.

3. Milk – Drinking milk can help boost your memory because it contains a wonderful substance called choline. As a writer, your memory is important; after all, you want the details in your story to be consistent. You don't want Mary to have blonde hair on page 3 and then brown hair on page 7.

4. Glucose – Foods that contain fructose can help your concentration remain solid. Avoid the high fructose corn syrup or alternative sweeteners. Stick to healthier natural sugars such agave and stevia, or eat some fresh fruit.

5. Protein and Whole Grains – Protein and whole grains are essentials for keeping your body energized and healthy. Your best bet is to eat a big breakfast that contains these nutrients. For example, try chowing down on some whole grain toast and an egg.

6. Supplements – In some cases you can take supplements to help boost your energy and mental clarity. Supplements come in all types, such as fish oil, multi-vitamins, individual vitamins, and minerals such as calcium with magnesium.

Choose Your Emotional Drivers

Before you start writing your story, you need to decide what you want your readers to feel when they read it. These will become your **emotional drivers**. To help you choose primary emotional drivers for your book, here is a brainstorming exercise:

Open up a word document and start writing down a long list of emotions. Include any feelings you want. Once your list is complete, narrow it down to two or three items. Select one primary emotion that is relevant to your genre. For example, a romance story would probably have physical sex as its main emotion, whereas a memoir could have a main emotion of depression. The other emotions on your short list can be used to provide variety and depth to your main character.

Romance itself, without the sex, is another type of emotion you could (and should) include in your romance story. Romance is the emotion of love without the physical aspects. However, you *can* carry the emotions from romance into a physical love scene.

Kick Start Your Creativity

In this final preparatory step, in order to start writing you will need to get your creativity going. Writer's block is often a writer's worst nightmare. No feeling is worse than getting everything ready, sitting down at your desk and then realizing you don't have a clue of what you're doing. However, writing something, *anything* every day is important. Your body, mind, and spirit need the repetition. I highly recommend that you pick a designated time to write something and follow it every day; after you have done this consistently, your body and your mind will accept the activity as a habit, and you will suffer less mental resistance to writing than if your schedule were haphazard.

One of the most popular ways to meet this requirement as well as motivate yourself to work on your main story is **freewriting**. Freewriting is and activity where you sit down and write whatever comes into your head. For freewriting to work best, you should set a limit, say, three minutes or three hundred words. This way you won't get lost in time, neither will you wear yourself out. Challenge yourself to write straight through without going back and making changes. If you really want to challenge yourself, close your eyes and don't look at what you've written until your time is up.

Another effective creativity strategy is to randomly pick a handful of letters from the alphabet and use those letters to create a potential title for a book. Then go ahead and start writing that story. Your tale can be as short or as long as you want. This strategy can serve as a warm-up to your writing project, or it could even turn into a full-length novel if you like the idea well enough.

If you're feeling really unmotivated, you could use a few "story starters" as a warm-up prompt. Creative Writing Now.com has some good writing prompts and story starters you can pick from to get started.

If you have already completed a book or a short story, a great creative writing strategy is to make up an alternative ending. Think about one of your favorite movies where they show another ending if you watch through the credits. If your story has a happy ending, maybe you could write up a more depressing ending. If your story has a sad ending, you can put a happy spin on it.

Alternatively, I sometimes find inspiration by reading one of my favorite authors' works, by watching a movie I've never seen before, or by playing a new role-playing game. I think that when I explore new experiences I am reminded that the creative possibilities out there are endless. This alone will often fire me up to get started writing again.

Never Say Never

Finally, never say you can't write romance. It's not easy but it can be done. You will need to utilize time, patience, determination and much practice, but with perseverance, you *can* master this form of writing. Every successful romance writer was at one time an inexperienced beginner. Keep going, keep learning, and eventually you too can reach the top.

Chapter 2: Story Basics

You now know what you can do to prepare yourself to write a killer romance story, but that was just the tip of the iceberg. As you delve deeper into planning and writing your story, you will soon discover there are a few additional "basics" to figure out before you can progress to a smooth and successful writing experience. In this chapter, you will discover all the details you must smooth over before you write your first chapter. Once you have these details figured out, writing your romance will come as easy as ever!

What is a Story?

A story develops when characters want what they can't have; usually, this will involve them in some sort of **change**. Readers generally like to see your main character change and grow across the life of the story. This change should be realistic, because your readers will be experiencing it through the eyes of your main character. When your protagonist begins to view one aspect of his life or his world differently, or when he gains a fresh insight into himself, a genuine shift in character will occur, which helps shape the end of your story. As your main character experiences growing discomfort – or a cataclysmic event – he is often pushed into an internal confrontation, which generates **conflict**. Alternatively, the conflict may occur first, driving your character toward internal change. As the main character undergoes change, this process will help shape your **plot.**

Why Write *This* Story?

Is your story intended to educate your readers? Are you writing purely to entertain? Are you trying to persuade them? Many stories within the categories of historical or military romance are almost automatically educational. Other educational novels provide an inside look at human nature. Stories based on social issues are easily persuasive in nature. Romance stories are generally meant to entertain your readers. Since the majority of romance novels end with the hero and heroine uniting, the main reason people read romances is to experience the same emotional rollercoaster your characters go through to reach that end. No matter your purpose, the most important thing to determine next is what subgenre is most effective for your story.

Romance Subgenres

If you're going to write a romance story, it is very important to understand what subgenre it will fall under. Though romance is about the relationship between a hero and heroine, it is also a very broad category where almost anything can happen. This is why it is important to know your subgenre; the subgenre will help you identify your target audience and, if you choose to go this route, potential publishers. Here is a list of the most popular subgenres of romance:

Contemporary Romance – Modern-day romance stories are set after both world wars. These stories contain a mixture of suspense, comedy, drama or other elements. The typical length for a contemporary romance novel is between 40,000 and 70,000 words.

Romance Anthology – Romance anthologies are sets of three or more novellas, which share a single theme. The majority of romance anthologies focus on historical times. If you are new to romance writing, you may want to develop your basic romance writing skill-set before setting out to write a romance anthology. The typical length for <u>each book</u> within an anthology is 25,000 to 35,000 words.

Fantasy Romance – Fantasy romance is a story set in another world or realm that revolves around a central love story. These stories often contain magical elements, mythological creatures or other fantasy-based characters. A fantasy romance novel runs somewhere between 70,000 and 120,000 words.

Romantica – Erotica romance stories contain heavily graphic details of meaningful sexual encounters between the hero and heroine, focusing very little on other characters. Typically, the heroine does not have sexual encounters with anybody other than the hero. The length of these books can range from 25,000 to 75,000 words.

Glamour Romance – Glamour romance stories focus on characters who are rich, powerful, elite and/or celebrities. This type of romance can run from a short length of approximately 7,000 words to a full-fledged novel with upwards of 70,000 words.

Chick-Lit – Chick-lit focuses on younger heroines who are usually in their twenties. These women tend to live in the present and, instead of searching for a hero to live happily ever after with, are known for impulsive decision-making and the inclusion of friends and family in their lives. Some may argue that chick-lit is not even romance subgenre at all, because it doesn't always follow the romance guidelines. For example, a chick-lit novel is likely to have an unhappy ending.

Ethnic Romance – Ethnic romance focuses upon heroes and heroines from a different culture than is represented in most Caucasian-based fiction. Most common ethnic subgenres include African American Romance literature or Latino romances. Publishers of ethnic romance novels often prefer the author to be of the same ethnicity as the characters. However, writers from any culture can publish ethnic romances if they do thorough research. In ethnic romance, color or culture does not necessarily have to be linked to the conflict. The length of books within this genre can range anywhere from 50,000 to 100,000 words.

Erotica – Erotica is a story that contains explicit and graphic details of sexual encounters. These encounters may exist between the hero and his heroine or between any other characters. These sexual encounters contain little to no aspects of romance. The length for erotica can range from 7,000 to approximately 25,000 words.

Sci-Fi Romance – Although a much smaller subgenre, sci-fi romance often focuses on the paranormal or time-travel. for the length of sci-fi romances can range between 75,000 and 100,000 words.

Romantic Suspense – Romantic suspense focuses on a love story in which the hero and heroine are involved in a dangerous or life-threatening situation or mystery. What makes romantic suspense differ from general suspense novels that have a romantic subplot is that the heroine is also directly involved in the action. In these stories, a dangerous situation causes the hero and heroine to fall in love, after they work together to defeat the antagonist. One challenge with this type of story is to balance the amount of suspense with the elements of romance. The length of romantic suspense novels ranges from 75,000 to 100,000 words.

LGBTQ Romance – LGBTQ romance focuses primarily on relationships between members of the same sex. Other than the fact that the hero and heroine are of the same gender, LGBTQ romance follows the five key elements of romance writing.

Historical Romance – Historical romance stories are set in historical times, ranging anywhere from ancient civilizations through the Second World War. Conflicts between hero and heroine must fit within this setting. Research and accuracy are important to make these types of stories believable The length of a historical romance novella can range between 25,000 and 35,000 words, and between 80,000 and 120,000 words for a novel.

Regency Romance – Regency romance focuses on stories set in England during the 1800s and tends to focus on the relationship between characters and the surrounding Victorian society. Regency romance shares a similar word count with historical romance.

Inspirational or Christian Romance – Inspirational romance focuses on the hero and heroine's relationship – or lack thereof – along with help from a higher power. Most inspirational romance features Christian characters, although any religion may figure in the setting. A typical conflict in inspirational romance is when one character believes in faith while the other does not. Another typical theme is where one of the main characters struggles to discover or return to the faith. Writers of inspirational or Christian romance should avoid using God or other religious figures as a supernatural solution to the conflict. Most readers like it when the characters work out their own solutions. The average length for an inspirational or Christian romance is usually between 50,000 and 100,000 words.

Medical Romance – Medical romances usually feature a conflict that involves some aspect of the medical profession. At least one of the main characters should have a career in medicine. The story should also focus on medicine as well as love and romance.

Young Adult Romance – These are romance stories focused on teenagers and young adults. The stories contain low levels of sensuality. They are becoming increasingly popular among younger readers. The length of a young adult romance can be 10,000 or more words.

Choose your Setting

It is important to choose the **setting** of your book early on, because it will serve as the world in which your story plays out. One of the best things about a setting is that it can range from plain and simple, to highly complex. In romance writing, your setting can help set the overall tone of the story. Defining the mood and the atmosphere of your setting is important to serve as a foundation for the emotional drivers of your story. Don't let laziness turn the setting of your romance novel into a cliché, such as the tropical romantic beach at night or the brooding mansion before a roaring fireplace. A clearly established setting with appropriate details will lay the groundwork for a well-rounded romance.

One factor to consider early on is your chosen subgenre. For example, if your story falls under the category science fiction, it would make a difference whether your story was set on the earth, on another planet or in a spaceship. If your story falls under historical romance subgenre, it would be unrealistic to set it on a spaceship. Instead, you have the fun of choosing between a medieval village, a Roman villa and a Renaissance religious community. Sometimes, the subgenre has no profound effect on the setting. LGBTQ romance, for example, contains few restrictions on setting. You can place your story on a spaceship, in a village, or anywhere you want, as long as it fits the context of the story.

Some writers like to set their romance stories in their hometown, or in a place they've visited and know well. In other cases, the storyline itself will suggest a setting. For example, if your storyline concerns two soldiers who fall in love, it would make sense to set your story on or near an army base.

It is ultimately up to you to choose your setting. The best advice I can give you is to be creative within your subgenre's restrictions, fill your setting with realistic details and paint it as vividly as possible for your reader.

The possibilities are truly endless when it comes to picking a setting. Here are some points to consider:

Universe/World – Will your story take place right here on Planet Earth, or will it be set in another realm?

You can place your story anywhere you want, and you can make the setting as broad or as localized as you choose. You can place it nearby or in a foreign culture, in a big city, a small town, on a beach, or even in the middle of an ocean. Would you rather restrict your setting to a small town or a specific neighborhood? Your setting can be as specific as a certain street, house, or building. It can also range as widely as the universe. Setting your story in a completely different universe or another imagined world is most common for fantasy or science fiction romances.

Time and Date – Setting a clear era for your book to inhabit will help your readers visualize the story. Some authors choose to draw out a timeline in their books, but that step is optional. However, it is important to state or at least hint at the age in which your book is set so that readers have an idea of how your characters will dress, act, and talk. Once you have set your timeframe, you will need to check periodically for time discrepancies. For example, if your book is set in the 1950s, your characters cannot just whip out their cell phones and exchange phone numbers. Especially when I am writing historical romance, I like to use actual dates in my chapter names, to give my readers a feel for the passage of time.

It is sometimes of key importance to tell or imply what time of day a scene takes place. I would, however, avoid an opening line like Snoopy's, "It was a dark and stormy night." Surely you can utilize your descriptive skills to *show* what's going on rather than overtly *tell* it. Here is an good example of implying a setting: "Johnny slid in the fresh dew that lingered on his front lawn as he chased after his wife." The start of a chapter or a section is a good place to clue in your readers regarding how much time has elapsed since the previous section. Once again, use your descriptive skills to weave implications into your text.

Atmosphere – Describing the atmosphere of your setting helps to set the moods within your story. You can use the weather or the lighting or some other external factor to set the mood, but do so sparingly. I've heard that publishers are turned off by stories that start with a description of the weather. Work the atmosphere into your story by describing it rather than *telling* the details. For example, if the atmosphere is intended to be sensual and romantic, instead of saying, "The heroine laid on the bed as she waited for her hero to join her,", you could more tactfully say your main character "waited anxiously as her fiancé moved about the room, lighting candles and spreading rose petals around the bed."

Geography – The geography of your setting can help frame the action in your story. Geography includes climate, plant life, bodies of water, and other land masses. Perhaps your main character goes to the beach every day until she meets her true love. I didn't think geography mattered at first, but it really does, even in romance. Your characters that live near the beach probably have a very different lifestyle from the mountain dwellers.

Historical Context – If your story revolves around an important historical event, such as a war or a tsunami, include that event in your setting. This will anchor the story in time for your readers; it also helps fit your book into the historical fiction genre, if this is your objective.

Politics, Economics, Sociology, Religion – These factors play into your setting and can dramatically affect the behaviors and the personality of your characters. A character who lives in the projects will act differently from one who lives in an affluent neighborhood. Likewise, a character who is a practicing Catholic could well have different reactions from one who is an agnostic. Considering these factors can also help you with set up the conflict. You have a built-in conflict brewing if your character is raised in a high-status background, but finds himself living in a slum. Alternatively, your agnostic character who finds herself forced to attend a Catholic school will be in for an experience she can either embrace or reject. Brainstorm some ideas surrounding these contexts and see what conflicts or plot twists you can come up with.

Your book's physical setting can be complex, affecting even minor details such as mannerisms, food or language. Setting can also be effective when it is kept to a few stark specifics. You can use subtle or lavish amounts of imagination, although I personally prefer the risk of erring in excess.

Research your world thoroughly, if you're not creating it from scratch. For example, if you plan to set your story in New York City, I highly recommend spending at least a day there to get a feel for what goes on, in addition to looking it up in newspaper articles and YouTube videos. Even if you are from New York and know every borough intimately, I suggest you take a day to play tourist, giving yourself a chance to view the old and familiar through fresh eyes.

What Makes Your Story Interesting?

One of your goals as a writer should be to write a story that will stand out and grab the interest of your readers. Picture them picking up your book and just dying to turn each page to find out what happens next. However, for that to happen, your book must be interesting, with fully fleshed out characters and a well-rounded story arc.

First, you should consider the plot. What is your plot? What kind of plot twists do you want to use? A good plot contains **exposition** (background descriptions to set the story and introduce the plot), **rising action** (the events, conflicts, twists and turns that lead to the high point of the story), a **climax** (the high point, where conflict elements really hit the fan), **falling action** (resolution of ongoing conflicts, filling in gaps that would otherwise leave your audience hanging in suspense) and a **resolution** (bringing the story to a satisfying end).

Plot in a romance story is often written in third person to let reader into hero and heroine's mind. Sometimes the plot is written from the heroine's first person point of view in chick lit and new adult. First person can limit details. Another option is dual first-person, which tells the story through both the hero and heroine's eyes. You can indicate which character is speaking by including their names on each chapter. Dual first person requires each character to have a unique voice.

Additionally, your story should have an early **hook**, something to swiftly engage your reader and make them want to read more. I've been advised to open my stories with some sort of disturbance, because a well-written disturbance automatically piques reader curiosity and raises questions about the back-story, the characters, and their motives. Your hook can be as intense as two lovers engaged in domestic violence, but it may also appear in more subtle form, such as a distressed mother trying to calm a crying baby. One way to determine if your story has a good hook is to see if it leaves readers wanting to know what happens next. For example, a book that opens up with a crying baby would probably make readers ask, "What is causing the baby to cry and how will the mother, who is seemingly stressed out and under pressure, react?"

Create a Plot Twist

A **plot twist** is essential to sustaining reader interest. You want to ensure that your story is not boring. Subsequently, you'll want to avoid creating an incredibly unbelievable plot twist that your readers won't buy. So, how do you go about creating a good plot twist? When one friend was writing her first novel, she was stumped for the longest time about how to make her story intriguing. Then one day, as she was taking a walk, a plot twist just popped into her mind out of nowhere. Some writers get lucky that way, but if your plot twist doesn't come to you like a gift, I have a few exercises that may help stimulate some ideas.

One powerful exercise is to brainstorm a list of possible–and impossible–plot twists. Write at least ten ideas if not more. Consider each idea, no matter how implausible, because even crazy ideas can sometime spawn brilliant ones.

Another suggestion is to read your story, looking for any scenes that might contain potential clues to a plot twist. For example, my friend originally wrote a scene in which her two main characters, a pair of former lovers, met up on a street corner, after having no contact for over three years. During their conversation, the female character mentioned she had some news to share. However, before she had a chance to let it out, the two got into an argument and the woman left without revealing her secret. That scene contained plenty of wiggle room for the author to experiment with until she could figure out how to use the untold secret as the setup for a major plot twist.

It helps to develop two or three plot twists that lead into each other. An easy way to do this is to follow a basic **three act structure** for your book. In this structure, your story will have a beginning, middle, and an end. Set your hook and create tension in at the very start with the first twist, using any type of challenge, obstacle, or disturbance. In this section, make extensive use of exposition and dialogue to introduce your readers to the setting and the main characters.

In the middle of your story, insert another twist. Make this plot twist a little more dramatic than the first one. Let this plot twist serve as the "point of no return" for your main character. Once he or she encounters this twist, there is nowhere to go but ahead. Make this plot twist life-changing. This part, the middle of your book, should take up the majority of your content.

Near the end of the middle section, insert your third plot twist, which will lead directly to the climax, which will lead to the resolution. This challenge or obstacle should ultimately lead to the resolution of all the individual threads in your story. In the climax, your protagonist will often be called on to make some sort of decision. In many stories, this twist will set up the final confrontation, either between two characters or within the main character. You must clearly show whether or not your main character has accomplished the goal set out earlier in the book. You may choose any type of ending. Although many readers look forward to a happy ending, sometimes your story will call for one that is sad or bittersweet.

Sometimes it can be difficult to keep your plot twists a secret until they actually occur. The You Tube video, Keeping the Plot Twist Secret by M. KIRIN provides some insight to this.

Conflict

Conflict is the single most important factor in romance writing. Most romance stories end with the hero and heroine living happily ever after, but the fun of watching the two overcome obstacles and barriers is what keeps readers going till the end. There should be conflict scattered throughout the story. Your hero and heroine should have at least one internal conflict. The main conflict in a romance story should be about the relationship status between the hero and heroine. The internal conflicts of each character can put the relationship at risk, linking it to the main conflict.

The conflict also has to be about something huge, not over a triviality. For example, conflict in a romance novel could consist of two lovers who disagree on where to buy a house, whether they should buy a house, or if they'd best just live in a trailer. More examples can include families not getting along, conflicts with careers, past hurt, betrayal, losing friends, or fearing change. Many times, love is what drives a conflict. For example, a young mother loves her family so much that she might not want her husband to continue his dangerous and risky career as a firefighter. Conflict can also stem from good intentions. For example, a man who is too protective of his woman might take it too far by cutting her off from her family, even though he doesn't see it that way. Avoid conflicts that take from away the from character's internal conflict, which is where most romance readers focus their attention.

For more tips on conflict in romance, check out the YouTube video, <u>Research & Writing Tips: How to Establish Romantic Tension in a Romance Novel</u> by eHow.

Inference

Narrative summary, a simple recitation of actions and the explicit statement of emotions or motives, makes for a boring, flat novel. If you leave nothing unsaid, you will be cheating your readers' imagination. The most important rule in romance writing is **show, don't tell**. Let your readers exist inside the story, viewing their surroundings as they view real life. In real life, nobody is handed all the information at once; most of the time, we have to infer motives and emotions by observing the circumstances in our larger environment. For example, take a look at the two passages below and ask yourself which one sounds better:

Passage A – It was John and Heather's first wedding anniversary and he wanted to make it a special occasion for his wife. However, Heather wasn't always the easiest person to please. Doing something special for her would be a challenge. After thinking it through all week, John finally came up with a great idea. He patiently waited for his wife to walk through the door, nervous about whether she'd like it. To his dismay, she didn't like it.

Passage B – The calendar on the wall over John and Heather's bed had a big, red heart drawn in one of the boxes. Looking at it, John smiled sentimentally, shifting his gaze to his and his wife's wedding photo on the nightstand. He was determined to make their first wedding anniversary special. All day, John went to great lengths to prepare for the moment. He picked out Heather's favorite bottle of wine, caressing its smooth surface as he set the table with her favorite flowers. He went so far as to scatter lighted heart-shaped candles throughout the house, which filled the rooms with a relaxing ocean scent. As the time drew near, John seated himself on the couch to wait for Heather's arrival. He fidgeted nervously, wiping sweaty hands and fussing with his necktie. A lump as big as a baseball formed in his throat when he heard her footsteps approach the door. He looked up, watching intently as Heather entered the room and stood, gazing neutrally at the table with its flowers and wine glasses, then surveying the gleaming candles. Try as he might, John could not discern even the slightest flicker of a response, and his hopes sank lower than the petals that lay scattered over the soft carpet.

Both passages made available the basic facts. However, the second paragraph sounds a lot better, right? You can actually feel the nervousness and tension of the main character through the description of his physical actions. As you read about him fidgeting on the couch, sweating and fussing with his tie, you actually start to feel the tension along with the character. You have successfully put yourself in the character's shoes.

I'll bet the second paragraph also held your interest a lot better than the first one. Readers don't want to read something that is long, boring and dragged out. Think of it this way: If you were a college student, would you select a class under a professor who stands in front of the class and speaks in a monotone, or would you prefer one who moves around and puts some zest into his lecture?

Notice how the second paragraph employs multiple senses in its description of the action. Touch, taste, sight, sound, and smell are powerful senses in real life; they can be just as useful when writing a story. Take note of how I used the senses of sight and smell to enhance the second paragraph. If you were to use taste, you could take a flat sentence like "the chocolate cake with vanilla icing tasted good" and turn it into "Warm, gooey chocolate dripped out of the freshly baked cake as it sat on the platter, waiting to be topped off with sweet vanilla icing." Which sentence makes your mouth drool?

Mechanics are Important

Use correct spelling, Standard English grammar, and appropriate punctuation in your story. Exceptions are only allowed when slang phrases suit your environment or when you have a character who speaks with an accent. There's nothing more annoying than trying to read a book with multiple errors; every mistake is a slap in the face of a reader. Always pay a proofreader to take a last look at your work before sending it off; you need a fresh set of eyes to see what you can't and the small price is well worth paying for the peace of mind you gain.

If you plan to publish your tale as an eBook, take the time to ensure that your book is formatted correctly for all platforms. Again, there's nothing worse than downloading a book and not being able to read it smoothly on your screen. Improper formatting only makes your text harder to follow; you also run the risk of your readers requesting a refund and leaving a bad review in their wake.

Sexual Tension

Building sexual tension in your romance story is a top priority. Sexual tension is the anticipation of sex, not the act itself. An excellent way to build sexual tension is to give your two main characters a strong mutual physical attraction, but also provide reasons why they can't act upon their desires. At least one character should be reluctant to go through with the act. You can build suspense through sexual tension by allowing it to appear in small bursts. For example, start with your characters staring into each other's eyes, then touching lips until the heroine suddenly pulls back, breaking the moment. Next time, you can let them go a little further and keep doing this until the act finally occurs. Avoid over-using clichés such as the interrupting phone call. Instead, focus on why the one character is so hesitant.

There are many different levels of sex that you can choose to include in your story, ranging from innocent romance – light kissing and holding hands – to graphic sexual descriptions.

The lowest level does not include anything physical beyond than a brief kiss or a light non-erotic touch. For example, a romance story between two teenagers may only include these details. As the level of sexual involvement increase, so does the level of detail in your description.

Subtle sex usually just involves foreplay and more kissing. You can choose for your love scenes to be purely sensual, meaning that your readers know your characters are having sex, but you draw the curtain on the scene without revealing any details. This type of sex is usually best suited for couples who are deeply and emotionally connected.

The next level is **steamy sex**. This kind of sex scene includes mildly graphic details and does not require the couple to have an emotional connection. Characters who engage in this type of sex usually end up staying together at the end of the story, even though their story may have started out as a simple hook-up.

Finally, **erotica** tops the chart of explicitness. Erotica includes graphic sex scenes in their most detailed form. Characters in an erotica book do not necessarily display even a spark of love. The book usually just focuses on two characters having sex with little to no storyline. Erotica can even include more than two characters in sexual activity, simultaneously. As the writer, you can let your imagination run without limits when writing erotica.

Finding Your Niche Audience

Romance is such a broad and appealing category of fiction that you can't just write a "romance" story. There are all sorts of romance readers in the world. Some prefer true stories that contain only subtle sexual references. Others prefer sensual sex while a few readers go after hardcore erotica that has little to no storyline. Some readers enjoy historical romances, others prefer paranormal romance. Some readers want a strong, alpha male lead and others want to read about a powerful female; readers have a wide range of preferences. As you can see, there are so many potential components to romance writing that it is simply impossible to write a story for "everyone." However, there is one key you can use to narrow down your audience.

First, ask yourself which factors of romance your book **emphasizes.** For example, if your story is a romance surrounded with a mystery and the core plot focuses on the latter, you are probably going to attract mystery-lovers as opposed to romance readers. If your book is sensual and contains many graphic depictions of sex, you are probably better off marketing to those who strictly enjoy erotica.

Next, ask yourself about your hero and heroine's core conflict. How **intense** is it? This measurement is useful for trying to guess which gender will want to read your book. Men tend to prefer conflicts that are full of action, adventure, danger and passion. Women may enjoy a conflict that is more emotional. Note that these preferences are generalizations; however, knowing what the majority likes is helpful for reaching the most readers.

Once you have established these elements, I recommend creating an **Ideal Reader Profile.** An ideal reader profile can help you capture a general picture of your average reader and you can use this to ensure that you've covered every element of your story before publishing. Creating an ideal reader profile for a romance novel is easy because there are many established statistics on who reads romance.

A study conducted by the Romance Writers of America in 2005 found that 64.6 million Americans read a romance novel at least one time that year. The same association found that 84% of romance readers are female while only 16% are male. Half of all romance readers reported to be married and half of all readers hold a bachelor's degree while a quarter have at least one graduate degree. On a broad spectrum, romance readers range from thirteen to over seventy five years of age, but of the majority of romance readers consist of women aged twenty-five to forty-five.

As you can see from these statistics, writing romance stories enables you to attract a wide female audience. Romance tales have impacted women throughout the years. For example, long before divorce was accepted by society, romance stories showed that sometimes divorce is easier and more logical than trying to maintain a dangerous and destructive relationship. Romance novels can also portray the importance of financial independence by featuring working women whose sexual relationship is just a pleasant add-on. Other romances affirm life lessons, such as "good men are worth waiting for" or "men should respect women."

Chapter 3: Romance Your Characters

Most romance authors focus on character development before thinking about the plot. Doing so is extremely important when writing romance, because it's the characters who make your romance story unique and who drive your plot forward. Creating a single character from scratch can be challenging, because the characters are the biggest influence in the story. If you don't already have an idea for your character or if you're not sure where to begin, you can use some archetypes to get started.

There are generally two main characters in a romance story: the hero and the heroine. One is usually the protagonist and the other is the love interest. It is more common for the heroine to be the protagonist, although a romance can also work the other way round.

Choose Your Major Characters

How many characters belong in one story? There really is no concrete answer. For a romance, you'll need two characters at minimum, the protagonist and the love interest. Sometimes the antagonist is set as the love interest. Your antagonist can also be an outside, third party. Let's learn more about the different characters you should include in any fiction book:

Protagonist

Your protagonist is the hero or heroine of your book, also known as a central character, major character, a dynamic or a round character. This main character must be one with whom your readers can identify. A protagonist is never perfect; in fact, your character's flaws are often what create the story's conflict. You will probably put a lot of effort into creating and understanding your protagonist. He or she must be as true-to-life as possible; after all, this is who your readers will follow throughout the entire story. Let your central character develop and grow across the span of your story. Readers like to watch a protagonist undergo substantial change; this is what they experience in their lives. Keep in mind that your readers are often drawn to a book because they are hungry to learn how another person solved a problem that is similar to their own.

I find that making your protagonist as true to life and as detailed as possible can help bring him or her to life. I do this by answering as many questions as possible about my protagonist. For example, I ask myself:

- Where does my character live? With whom does she live?

- What type of dwelling does she live in? How did she come to live there? Does she like it?

- Where is she originally from? What is her background?

- How old is my protagonist? (This is a very important question, because it determines so many other details).

- What is my protagonist's name? How does this reflect her personality, her background, and possibly, the challenge she will face in this book?

- What is the social class of my protagonist?

- What does my protagonist look like? (The more details you write, the better a description you will get).

- What was her childhood like and how does it affect her now?

- What does my protagonist do for work? Does she work at all?

- How does my protagonist handle change/conflict?

- What kind of relationships does she have?

- What is her goal?

Let these questions branch off into sub-questions. For example, when you ask yourself about your protagonist's childhood, explore whether she was raised by a single mother, by an abusive father, or by adoptive parents. By answering these questions, you are creating a solid framework for your book. For example, if you decide that your protagonist is a sixteen-year-old girl, you wouldn't write a scene with her drinking in a bar unless you're painting her as a defiant teen. Avoid letting your protagonist live an unchanging and boring life; otherwise you will not hold your readers' attention long enough to reach the checkout lane.

Describe Your Protagonist Early

It is crucial for your readers to get acquainted with your protagonist early in the story; otherwise, they will be less likely to identify places where inner growth and change may occur. Think of your story's beginning as a snapshot of your protagonist in his or her "lost" state. Ensure that your readers understand who your protagonist is at the beginning, so they will better comprehend the changes, challenges, sacrifices, and obstacles he will go through en-route to becoming a more "complete" person. For example, let's review the storyline from the movie *Shrek*. In the beginning, Shrek was a miserable, lonely monster who had no friends and projected a generally negative attitude. However the events, challenges, and friendships he experienced had changed him into a happily married, positive-thinking monster by the resolution. The ending wouldn't have been significant at all if Shrek had remained unchanged.

Here are some additional questions to focus on once you've settled on the basics of your protagonist:

- What goes on around your protagonist and what goes on inside her head as a result? In other words, which external factors act as a stimulus for which internal factors? If your protagonist is a generally moral person but she loses her home and is forced to live under a bridge, where might that lead? The conflict between external circumstance and internal morals will be the drawing factor of your book. Your protagonist is faced with a choice: will she violate her morals by breaking the law to survive, something he would have never done earlier, or will he discover another way out of her dilemma?

- What will be the trigger that moves your protagonist to change? Perhaps she is required to overcome a specific character weakness in order to achieve "completeness." Another main character may suddenly, in an "aha" moment, discover she now knows what is happening or she now has what he needs to emerge from his difficulty. This sudden knowledge will often trigger your final plot twist and lead directly to the climax of your story.

- Why is it significant for your protagonist to reach "completeness?" To answer this question, think in terms of life lessons. Readers like to feel your story has a message; in many cases this theme will come in the form of a life lesson that becomes apparent by the resolution.

- What has to happen by the resolution in order to make your protagonist "complete?" The answer to this question is often a high-stakes climax followed by an engaging victory. Think of it as "the final standoff" or a life-changing event that firmly establishes the resolution.

- Does your protagonist gain redemption in the end? Will she be required to sacrifice something to reach her goal? Readers like to see a protagonist make a sacrifice, because it is inspiring. Your character gives up something she values in order to benefit somebody else.

Alternatively, your protagonist may be an **Anti-Hero**. An anti-hero protagonist does not have the traditional positive qualities of a regular protagonist and is often immoral, self-centered, or unheroic. Some anti-heroes have addictions or are involved in some sort of corruption. However, an anti-hero usually grows into a more complete person by the end, even though it often comes at the cost of his life. Anti-heroes often inspire readers to overcome their own insecurities.

A Well-rounded Protagonist

Good protagonists should contain enough detail of character to make them interesting individuals. Here are some points to consider:

First of all, your protagonist needs a **personality**; otherwise you're drawing with a white crayon on white paper, so to speak. You want your protagonist to jump off the page and into the hearts of your readers. The best way to create a strong personality is to answer as many questions as you can about his background. You'll want to be able to explain and predict your protagonist's thoughts and feelings.

Exercises

You can increase your personality development skills by participating in method acting classes or stream of consciousness exercises. The activity below may also be of help:

I'm a big fan of voice recorders; I think talking into a voice recorder as if you were your protagonist can be a very helpful creative exercise. To experience this exercise, begin by introducing yourself and then speak as if you were that character and see what comes out. Try this for at least ten minutes, since you will need a little time to get comfortable with the concept and really get into your character. Your brain could very well start making up things you think are genius. When you are finished, replay the tape to glean the best parts for your protagonist.

A good way to add some personality to your protagonist is to **exploit her fear**. Just because your protagonist isn't real doesn't mean she can't feel fear. We all have fears; just connect your protagonist's fears to the story line. This will help your character seem more real and believable. A fearless protagonist (unless it makes sense in the story) will all too often come across as robotic and nonhuman.

You also need to decide what your protagonist's **internal conflict** will be. Internal conflict is when your character wants two things but is unsure which one to pick or how to get both. The best way to capture your readers' attention and take them on a psychological joyride is to create an internal conflict that is emotional and testing. Try to stay near to a type of internal conflict you might find in yourself one day.

Once you've figured out the internal conflict, you'll also want to determine the **external conflict.** External conflict is driven by an outside factor that is somehow related to the internal conflict. For example, in the internal conflict, your protagonist has to pick between fleeing his hometown and remaining in an unhealthy and unsafe environment. If you add in an assassin who is chasing your protagonist, that will serve as your external conflict.

Next, your protagonist needs **motivation.** A character's motivation is usually connected to her values and ambitions as well as her goals. A good way to portray motivation in your story is to give your protagonist two clashing values, which will create internal conflict; then your character will be forced to pick between them. Ambition, which represents what your protagonist wants more than anything, will be the driving motivation. Limit your protagonist's ambition to one thing. Her ambition will move her to choose between options and can be the driving force behind her actions.

Your protagonist should also have **relationships** with other characters in your story. Of course, the hero and heroine will have a special relationship; but all relationships can help push your story forward. Think about a hero and his friends or a heroine and her family members. Relationships make it possible for your protagonist to connect with your readers. Your audience wants to identify with the main character; that's one of the main reasons he or she is reading your book. For example, young adult books are specifically written for young adults, with characters of the same age who experience similar conflicts to the typical young adult.

Give your protagonist a unique **voice.** This often includes the way your character speaks and moves. For example, if your protagonist is a gangster, he might talk using jargon specific to gangsters and he may stalk rather than walk. If your protagonist is a professor of physiology, she would probably speak with advanced vocabulary and complex sentence structures. Giving your protagonist a unique voice helps establish your main character's personality. It can even reflect part of a backstory. For example, if your character stutters, his voice could link to a past that involved bullying or abuse.

Similarly, your protagonist should be full of **emotion.** An emotionless protagonist is worse than watching paint dry. For example, if your protagonist is in the middle of a break-up with someone else, think about what emotions will come into play. Often the other person will be extremely upset and will cry, beg, or otherwise try to convince your protagonist not to walk away. All the while, the main character is resistant to these emotions and just wants out of the relationship once and for all. In another scenario, think about all of the emotions present in a wedding scene. The feelings would be mostly positive, but think about a parent's objection or something else that could go wrong. Examine many possible scenarios and use their related emotions to your advantage when you write.

Give your protagonist at least one **strength** and one **flaw.** A protagonist with no strengths at all is pretty boring and one-dimensional. So is one with no flaws. What's the point of reading about your protagonist if he or she doesn't have anything human to offer or any space for growth? If you give your protagonist an amazing strength, also include a character flaw. The juxtaposition of these two character traits opens up all sorts of possibilities to generate conflict. For example, your character in a romance story could be a genius in the computer lab, but at the same time be horribly clumsy when it comes to dating.

What else makes for a good protagonist in a romance story? One key is the inclusion of a **mystery** or a **secret.** This works best if one character is already mysterious and another one has a secret; the secret may explain why the other character is so mysterious. For example, let's say you are writing a story about a love triangle, in which your protagonist skips town with the woman whom he regards as his soul mate, but he still stays in touch with his ex. The ex has a secret; she is carrying his child or she has some sort of incurable disease. The new girlfriend doesn't know this secret, so her boyfriend's mystique drives her crazy. If your readers don't know the secret either, they will be driven crazy as well and are all the more likely to read to the end of your book in their quest to uncover the secret.

The majority of readers like to see a protagonist with lots of courage, inner strength, sex appeal, mental sharpness, generosity, kindness, or selflessness. However, romance is fiction, so it's totally up to you and your story, what kind of person you want your protagonist to be. Of course, if your protagonist is an anti-hero, you won't make him selfless or genuinely caring.

One of the best things about fiction is that following these rules is somewhat optional. I say "somewhat" because you must know the rules thoroughly before you can understand when you can get away with bending, or outright breaking them. Nine times out of ten, it is best to stick closely to the rules if you want to be successful, but you know what they say about rules being built to be broken. There's really no straight-forward answer. You could play by the rules and write a flop; you could also deviate from them and discover you've captured your audience with a completely new concept.

While we have focused on developing a powerful protagonist you can apply all of these tools to your other characters; for a successful book, you need a well-rounded cast. If your protagonist is fully developed but is surrounded by flat, one-dimensional characters, you'll still have a weak storyline.

Antagonist

The antagonist is a character in your story that goes up against the protagonist. He or she usually stirs up conflict, sometimes just by entering the scene. In some stories the antagonist is very clear, but in others it's not as easy to pick out. Think of the antagonist as the personification of an obstacle your protagonist must overcome. Sometimes the antagonist is referred to as the **foil**, which describes a contrasting character, in terms of personal qualities.

Minor Characters

These are characters who assist in moving the story forward or serve as a contrasting personality. They can provide depth to more important characters by revealing aspects of backstory. **Stock Characters** are flat, stereotypical individuals who are easily identified, such as the mad scientist or the nerd.

However, use stock characters sparingly. A story peopled by stock characters can seem cartoonish and is difficult to elevate beyond boring.

One Main Question, One Main Goal

As I mentioned earlier, your story should have a single main question, which usually connects with the goal of your protagonist. For example, Indiana Jones usually goes off looking for treasure, which provokes the readers to ask, "Will he find the treasure?" Your story may generate multiple questions, but one should always be primary. In romance, the primary question is often, "Will the hero and heroine survive the challenges that prevent them from being happily together?"

To ensure that your round characters stay round, every character should have a goal. The most important goals are usually the conflicting objectives that strike sparks between your protagonist and antagonist. For example, Spiderman (the protagonist) wants to protect the city while the Green Goblin (the antagonist) wants to destroy him—and it. Spiderman also wants M. J. (a minor character) to fall in love with him, while she is more focused on becoming an actress. People who watch the movie find themselves asking questions about both unknowns. Notice how all three of these characters have goals that help move the story forward.

Character archetypes are stock characters who you often find in stories. The archetype is meant to give your character's personality a jump-start. By developing the character through his or her goals, motivation and conflict, you can turn the archetype into a unique person.
Here are the most common hero and heroine archetypes that you can use to start molding your characters:

Heroine Archetypes

Most romance stories focus on the heroine's story through her point of view. The heroine should be realistic, with good and bad qualities. An imperfect heroine will enable your readers to better identify with her. Her strengths and flaws should balance out one another. While you'll want to avoid creating a stunning, perfectly put together heroine who has her act together, you also don't want to have a "dumbed down" heroine who is incapable of caring for herself. Make sure that your heroine has a decent amount of self-respect.

Though it may seem shallow, your heroine should be regarded as attractive, especially to the hero. However, this includes mental attractiveness in addition to physical. Ask yourself this: Other than looks, what would make a man desire a woman?

When crafting your heroine, it is particularly important to pay attention to her backstory. Many people believe a backstory always has to be negative (for example, a heroine who is running from trouble) but that's not always the case.

Backstory simply sets the scene for your heroine. She is a person who has been shaped by past experiences. Think about factors such as her home life, parenting style, brothers or sisters, experiences in school and anything else that may play a role in shaping your present heroine.

I've always found it helpful to create a character's backstory all at once and then sprinkle it in throughout the story. Many first-time authors make the mistake of dumping the entire backstory in at once, usually in the beginning, and that can turn your readers away. It is much more exciting and suspenseful to learn more about your heroine little by little than it is to find out all at once.

Modern-day heroines are independent and self-sufficient. They tend to have their own careers and are able to support themselves. If your heroine has a less than fabulous job, such as a bartender, she usually has plans to improve her financial situation. Though she is mature and can make it on her own, she also has some problems, which may be a result of her backstory. A younger heroine may have created the problems she is facing. Don't make your heroine need a love interest but make her **want** one.

Having trouble figuring out where to start with your heroine? Here are some common archetypes you can use as a foundation:

The Boss – The alpha female; in charge and doesn't need help from a man

The Prep – Energetic, always happy, willing to do for others; has a hard time making decisions and is often in the middle of love affairs

The Advocate – More interested in promoting social justice than romance

The Cynical – Often a survivor and can tend to hide behind a mental wall and may have a mysterious attitude

The Free Spirit – Happy go lucky, marches to her own beat but hard to hold down

The Nanny – Always puts others before herself, shy and holds back; can sometimes come off as nosy

The Distressed Damsel – A women with secrets, may be running or hiding from something; often resorts to taking care of herself

The Intellectual – Often too "busy" for love, factual, can be intimidating to others

Hero Archetypes

While the majority of romance stories center on the heroine, the hero is just as important, because he is what the story revolves around. Therefore, it is extra important to develop a solid, intriguing hero that your heroine will be attracted to. Female writers especially, should be careful not to give the hero too many girly characteristics, otherwise he may not come off as the "right" type of hero and your audience will be dissatisfied. You should also ensure that your hero does not come across as forceful and abusive. give your characters a balance of personality traits.

Like your heroine, your hero has to be physically and mentally attractive, although mental attractiveness holds a little more weight for the hero. Your hero doesn't have to be a billionaire. If you are a female writer, give your hero traits and characteristics that would make him come off as a good husband. In romance, there are generally two types of heroes: Alpha and Beta. Alpha heroes tend to be more dominant and powerful while beta heroes tend to be casual and family-oriented. Both can be equally successful in your story. Experiment with each one to discover which type fits best in your romance.

Creating a backstory for your hero is a little different than when you do it for your heroine, due to the fact that men are less likely to dwell on their past. However, that doesn't mean a hero's past experiences have no influence on how he feels in the present. For example, heroes with commitment problems or guys who don't understand how to be supportive may have suffered something in the past that triggered this kind of response. The heroine of the story may be what inspires the hero to overcome his past and change for the better.

Having trouble figuring out where to start with your hero? Here are some common archetypes you can use as a foundation:

The Alpha Male – Displays a dominant and "in charge" attitude

The Bad Boy – Rebellious and does not play by the rules

The Best Friend – Sensitive, understanding and respectful

The Player – Charming, smooth talker, popular but hard to pin down

The Wanderer – Comes from a damaged past, emotionally distant, often keeps secrets

The Intellectual – Smart, factual and subsequently cold or unemotional

The Fighter – Stands up for things he believes in

One important note: Your heroine and love interest should grow as persons as your story progresses. To develop a couple that is perfect for each other; ask yourself some of these questions:

1. How do the strengths and weaknesses of your hero and heroine balance each other?

2. Are there any traits that would make them a terrible couple?

3. How do pet peeves affect your hero and heroine?

4. What are the significant differences between your hero and heroine?

For more tips on developing your main characters, check out the YouTube video, [Romance Authors: Creating Characters](), by oclsvideos.

Keep a Character List

I highly recommend creating and keeping a character list to prevent and eliminate inconsistencies. For example, if you write in the beginning that your character has brown eyes you don't want to describe her eyes as blue a few chapters later. A detailed character list that includes physical characteristics, mental traits and the personal background will remind you at a glance that your character has brown eyes. My artistic capability scarcely extends beyond stick figures, but if you can draw, I highly recommend setting down a highly detailed visual representation of your characters, especial the primaries.

Backstory

Alright, let's talk more about the backstory. Backstories can serve as a useful tool to flesh out your various personalities. A character's backstory is what helps your readers understand where he is coming from–quite literally, what causes her to drop to the ground whenever lightening explodes, or why he carries that enormous chip on his shoulder. It is essentially the history of your character. Although your protagonist's backstory is often the most important, all your characters can become more realistic if hints to their backstories are dropped periodically.

Also, don't make the mistake of turning your first few chapters into a backstory. A backstory is just that, an entirely separate story. Call it a prequel if you will, but only publish it *after* your current novel has become successful!

Flashbacks are a useful tool to reveal aspects of a character's backstory. I know one author who has utilized flashbacks to complement what she was actually writing and it worked out well. What she did was to start telling the main story about a girl who was kidnapped, then she sprinkled snippets of backstory throughout the book in the form of flashbacks. As you read through the book, you learn what the girl had been doing prior to being snatched, and you also discover why her abductors were so crazy as to nab her. flashbacks not only help round out the characters, they also keeps the readers' curiosity piqued for new information.

If you're going to use flashbacks to tell your story, be careful to transition smoothly back and forth between them and your story's present tense. One straightforward method is to start a flashback as a new scene, indicating it by using the simple past tense. When you end the flashback, close out the scene and switch back to the present tense, continuing the main story.

Backstories are flexible so you can create it up front or develop it as you go along. I find that having a general idea of a character's backstory is good enough for starters. You can flesh out the details as you write. Having a backstory all written out in front of you helps you keep track of your story's context. This is especially useful if you have an extensive backstory for multiple characters.

I recommend using backstory development as a warm-up for additional writing. Just select a character and start developing a backstory. Don't worry; your backstory can evolve as your story develops. Then, as you write your main book, you can decide what snippets or details from the backstory will help move your story forward.

Interior Monologue

Knowing how to use interior monologue (essentially getting into the head of your character) is useful is highly useful. There are two types of interior monologue, direct and indirect. Direct interior monologue is when your character is speaking directly from inside her head. Many authors use italics to indicate this. Let's look at an example of direct interior monologue:

"The only thing that could complete her day trip was if she had someone with her besides her boring parents. Anyone, really. A cousin, a friend…a boyfriend. *Like I'll ever have one of those.*"

Direct interior monologue is also best written in first person present tense, as you can see in the example above. Putting direct thoughts in italics helps them stand out to the reader. That being said, you should try to use italicized direct interior monologue sparingly, otherwise it will lose its special flavor.

Indirect interior monologue exists when the author tells you a character's inner thoughts as narrative description. Let's look at an example:

"Being home schooled was something that Emily didn't like to share. It embarrassed her to talk about it."

Sometimes, a tag, such as "he said" or "she thought" is necessary to keep straight who is thinking what. For example:

"*I have been angry ever since she left me*, he thought to himself."

Most authors I know use a mixture of direct and indirect interior monologue to reveal their characters' internal processing. People sometimes read fiction because the interior monologue enables them to see what a character is thinking, as opposed to guessing from the action, as in a movie.

Interior emotions can help develop your character. Interior emotion tells readers about your character by showing their emotions. For example, if your character is scared, you can describe the physical effects of fear, such as starting to sweat, or a racing heart. Don't come right out and say that he's scared. That's narrative summary, something I already warned you to avoid for the most part. If you are unsure how to work interior emotion into your scene, just ask yourself, "What is my character feeling and what does that look like?" Similes and metaphors can add power to your descriptions of interior emotion. Just use highly clichéd examples very sparingly.

Developing Character Through Dialogue

Dialogue is an extremely important element in fiction because it helps develop your characters and push your plot forward. That being said, the dialogue in your book must be perfectly crafted. Alfred Hitchcock once said that a good story is "life with the dull parts taken out." In other words, readers don't want to read something like this:

"What do you want to do today? Hook up?"
"Oh yeah, that sounds good."
"Okay, I'll go get undressed right now. Meet me in the bedroom."

Boring, right? Dialogue requires focus, impact and relevance to be effective. It needs to push your plot forward or reveal something about your characters For example, let's rewrite the above example to create some conflict and introduce tension between the characters:

"What do you want to do today?"
"How about something I want to do for once? You never let me pick."
"I never let you pick because I know what you ultimately want and it's wrong."

Dialogue Tips

I personally believe that writing good dialogue stems out of the "practice makes perfect" philosophy. The more you experiment with it, the more naturally your dialogue will sound. Nonetheless, here are some things to keep in mind when writing dialogue:

1. Don't give out too much information at once. Let tidbits slip out in normal conversation. If you try to force information on your reader, your

characters may sound stilted and you may find yourself overusing narrative summary. Instead, keep your dialogues short and succinct. Limit each dialogue to a single main thought. Try to restrict each character to about three lines of dialogue at one time.

2. Use context clues to hint at the topic of your characters' conversation. For example, if two characters are speaking about an awkward topic like breaking up, build the tension and discomfort of the scene by describing their body language, e.g., a male and a female lingering on the front porch, not saying much, keeping their arms folded. When the male eventually suggests, "What if we just tried living separately?" the dialogue will provide resolution of the tension.

3. Vary your format when creating dialogue tags. Avoid a series of, "He exclaimed," followed by "She sneered," "He gasped," and "She interjected." One way to tell if you're writing good dialogue is to ask yourself, "Will my reader know my character is acting surprised, angry, or hyper without me saying so in a tag?" The real purpose of a dialogue tag is to help your reader keep track of who is talking. The use of too many descriptive verbs in this situation can actually distract from the conversation.

If you can make it obvious which character is talking, then you do not need a tag at all. For example: "I can't believe he's late." Jessie continuously checked her watch. "He said eleven thirty." You also do not need tags if you indicate that two characters are speaking and then continue their conversation without an action break.

4. Do, however, break up your dialogue with action so that it does not run on too boringly. By doing this you can minimize dialogue tags while providing your reader with enough details for an accurate visualization.

5. Give your dialogue the correct punctuation. If you don't, your reader can easily become confused and give up on your book. Here are three simple rules to remember:

   - Always add a comma between the end of your dialogue and its tag line ("My parents are so lame," Emily said).

   - Keep the comma or period inside the quotation marks.

   - Use a comma at the end of the first part of an interrupted statement and another comma at the end of the tagline. ("I don't know," Emily said, "We'll just have to wait and see.").

Lovers in Conflict

Creating conflict between your hero and heroine is the heart of keeping readers interested in your story. However, you must develop your conflict carefully. There needs to be a problem, but not just any problem; it should be one that generates tension. Sometimes your problem can be challenging or confusing in order to create conflict and build tension. Here is a list of questions you can ask to measure the conflict you've developed:

1. Why would your hero and heroine be enemies?

2. What stops them from being friendly with one another?

3. What topics do they have differing opinions on?

4. What is at stake?

5. Why does the tension between them matter?

Avoid using simple challenges such as a fight, communication problems or other trivial issues. Use this rule of thumb: If the problem can be solved through an email or phone call, then it is not tense enough to be part of the main conflict.

There are two main kinds of conflict: **internal** and **external**, and in romance, you'll need to utilize both. The best romance stories feature internal and external conflicts that fit closely together. External conflict is a third-party problem that the hero and heroine have to face head on, for instance, family problems or living arrangements. A good way to identify the external conflict is to read the back or inside cover of a book, because it is usually written there as part of the hook. For example, the description of the book *Fifty Shades of Grey* tells of Anastasia, a young student, who meets a powerful entrepreneur during an interview. So in this case, the external conflict is that a naïve girl and a more intimidating man meet each other through something work-related. Internal conflict is the deeper struggle found within the hero and heroine. It usually consists of a weakness or an obstacle that is triggered by a past experience. The description goes on to describe the internal conflict of the hero and heroine in *Fifty Shades of Grey*: the student has to overcome her curiosity of the entrepreneur's erotic desires and he has to overcome his controlling nature.

Naming Your Characters

Naming your character is often a big deal. If your story blows up big, everyone will know your main characters by name. Some authors put great emphasis into naming their characters and others pick out names without much thought. Some authors like to reveal facts about their characters through their name or have their name represent something. In romance, naming your character also brings another magical element to the table: emotions.

If done correctly, the way a character says another character's name in a romantic setting can have a profound effect on your readers' emotions. Imagine the hero speaking the heroine's name for the first time with a sparkling smile on his face. Imagine him yelling it with rage in his eyes and balled firsts. Imagine him saying her name as he cries out in heartbreak. Continue imaging the exchange of names under different emotions. This can help give your readers a vivid visual of what's going on; it can also help move the plot forward or provide key revelations that affect the tension between your characters.

Here are some things to consider when picking out the names for your hero and heroine:

1. Sound and rhythm – Let's face it, some names are just better sounding than others. Some names just sound so dreamy that you can picture the most handsome or beautiful hero or heroine. This is where rhythm comes into play. When choosing a name for your hero or heroine, say it out loud and think about how rhythmic it sounds. Does it sound dreamy? Can you picture the most stunning person when you say it?

2. Keep unusual or unique names to a minimum. Otherwise, the names of your characters can get too confusing and it makes you seem like you're trying to be too original as an author. For example, if your heroine's name is Allegra, make your hero's name more common, such as Jim.

3. Double-check that your characters' names are relevant to their generation. This isn't always necessary but it can help your story feel more realistic. For characters that were born in the current generation, you can easily go online and look up the most popular names. Then you can search popular names for their parents' generation and assign those names to their parents or other older characters. This is an especially good idea if you're writing historical romance; it would sound "off" if you gave a character in the 1700s a name from this century. For historical romance, also research how social status can be revealed by a name.

Many writers keep a notebook of potential character names. This isn't a requirement, but I think it can help speed up the story planning process. You can also use a notebook to take notes on the names you've written down: what they mean, their origin, and how popular they are today.

Chapter 4: Romantic Story Goals

In romance, the hero and heroine both need motivating but conflicting goals. Each goal should have a high amount of importance to the character. Romance stories characters often create goals driven by fear. When building emotional conflict, try to select problems that are as realistic as possible. Romance readers will relate much better when you portray believable, real-life problems instead of unrealistic storylines.

The story goal for a hero or heroine is limited in a romance because there are only so many things that a character in this type of story can want. That being said, this enables authors to really get creative and give each story goal a twist. Most characters reach their goal after the inciting incident, although the goal can also have ties to the characters' backstory.

Here are some of the most popular story goals you can use in your romance story:

Find True Love

In nearly all romances, the main objective of the hero or heroine is to find true love. This desire usually stems out of his or her backstory. Perhaps he's been lonely his entire life or she never really had anybody to love her. When the hero or heroine finds true love, it often causes an internal change in the protagonist. For example, the movie *Shrek* is about a lonely, mean and pessimistic ogre but when he finds companionship in the princess, he realizes that all he needed was love and by the end of the story, he is happily married and no longer mean. When the hero or heroine searches for true love throughout the story, it usually results in marriage or the assumption of marriage. In other words, think of the "happily ever after" theme.

This story goal makes it necessary to truly exploit your characters' flaws. If two people are perfect for each other, then finding true love will be easy. However, the character flaws allow for some conflict, making the story interesting and the ending much more satisfying. Although most romance stories are told through the heroine's point of view, a hero can be looking for true love as well.

Solve Relationship Problems

In some romance stories, the hero or heroine wants to ultimately resolve his or her relationship problems. The story often starts off with a failing relationship with one of the main characters setting off on a mission to save the relationship before it's too late. The key is to ensure one character wants to save the relationship while the other is reluctant. The movie *Fireproof* portrays a good example of this goal in action. In the beginning the hero, Caleb, and his wife are just about to end a marriage that seems hopeless. They are both ready to give up, but Caleb's father challenges him to take one last shot at saving his marriage.

Throughout the story, the wife is unresponsive and unwilling to accept Caleb's actions, but after he commits a highly selfless act, she falls in love with him again.

The theme in stories centering on this goal often include "renewed love" or "character growth." In the case of the above example, the theme was about staying true to one's Christian faith. When the protagonist has achieved his goal, he and the heroine usually end up getting back together and presumably live happily ever after.

Overcome Forbidden Love

When something is forbidden, especially love, it tends to become much more desirable. In a story where the goal is overcoming forbidden love, the hero and heroine are attracted to each other but, for some external reason, cannot easily be together. This story goal has been around since Shakespeare wrote Romeo and Juliet, where the hero and heroine couldn't be together due to familial differences.

There are many reasons why a hero and heroine can't be together. There could be social class differences, racial differences, age differences, political differences or almost any kind of stark difference. My personal favorite romance movie is about a woman who falls in love with a criminal; she sacrifices the relationship, letting him go in order to protect herself and her son. Stories involving public servants also easily match this goal, because the main characters often disagree about a dangerous aspect of one's profession (e.g., the heroine is afraid of her hero fireman falling through a roof or her hero policeman getting shot on the job).

By the time you reach the resolution, the hero and heroine usually figure out how to be together. In the case of Romeo and Juliet, they chose death, but it isn't always necessary to go to that extreme. Sometimes the two simply have to wait for each other (reflecting the theme of "good things come to those who wait") or the two come to a compromise (one of them steps down from a dangerous job in favor of love). The key to this story goal is figuring out how the hero and heroine eventually come together in the end.

Win Back His Love/Find New Love

Another popular story goal in romance is for the protagonist to win back a lost love. In many cases, the heroine gives the hero an ultimatum. For example, stop smoking or end the relationship. In this case, the hero has to struggle through the change to win back his love. Although heroes can give the heroines an ultimatum, it is largely the other way around in most stories. Therefore, the hero's goal is to successfully change and reap the benefits.

Often, the change a hero experiences can adjust his life to the extent that he ends up with another woman. For example, in the movie *Big Daddy*, Sonny's girlfriend gives him an ultimatum: grow up and get serious about life or lose her. He adopts a child to show her he is mature and although it all goes wrong, his choices lead him to his true love and he ends up a responsible man in a great relationship.

If you decide to reunite the hero and heroine, then you can adopt the theme of "Change is for the better." If your characters find other partners along the way, you can rest on the theme of "Some things are meant to be."

Make the Partner Happy/Provide a Better Life

Sometimes, the goal of your protagonist can simply be to make the partner happy. For example, your hero and his wife might have a family but are struggling financially, so the hero sets out to find a way to make his family's life better. He could do things to improve himself and get into trouble along the way. Perhaps he makes a deal with the mafia or otherwise gets tied up in something illegal, then has to figure out a way to make things right all around. Sometimes your hero will end up sacrificing something – even a relationship – to see his partner happy or to let her live a better life.

Protect Each Other

Protecting each other can be an exciting story goal, especially for romantic suspense. Usually the hero has to keep the heroine safe although it can be the other way around. Often times, the hero and heroine meet each other as a result of a protection order and fall in love by the end. The stakes for protecting the heroine should be high, putting an immense amount of pressure on the hero.

Forgive and Be Forgiven

Forgiving or seeking forgiveness can be a story goal for either the hero or heroine. In a story with this type of goal, the hero or heroine has done something wrong, either to the partner or outside of the love interest's knowledgeOne way or the other, the hero or heroine pursues ultimate forgiveness and wants to figure out how to get it.

If you are having trouble coming up with a story goal, here are a few questions to ask yourself that might help:

- Why is this goal important to the main character?

- What will the goal prove?

- What values surround this goal?

- How does this goal reflect the hero or heroine?

- How will the hero or heroine emotionally respond to failure or a half success?

- Who will help him or her reach the goal?

- Does the goal involve a moral issue and how will that affect the hero or heroine?

- Will the character need to sacrifice anything to reach the goal?

- Will he or she need to accomplish anything to reach the goal?

- Once the goal is completed, will it lead to another goal?

- Will the goal become increasingly urgent as the story draws to an end?

- Does the goal trigger any fears?

- What gets in the way of the hero or heroine achieving the goal?

- How does the goal contribute to character growth?

- Does the goal reflect a strength or weakness in your hero or heroine?

- Does your hero or heroine develop strength to finally achieve the goal?

Chapter 5: Romantic Outlines

Writing a book can be overwhelming, especially if it's your first time. However, you can pretty easily get a handle on the big picture and maintain continuity across hundreds of pages, by using outlines. I recommend that you outline not just the story itself, but each major aspect: the plot, your characters, the chapters, and the scenes within those chapters. With these aspects clearly outlined, you are able to easily access and reference the most important parts of your story.

While some writers depend heavily upon outlining to get them through the writing process, others hate outlines and firmly resist their use. Managing via outlines is a personal preference, but I think you can benefit from this discipline, especially in the beginning. Don't begrudge yourself the time it takes; the process of outlining multiple aspects of your story will actually help ensure you don't miss important details. By the time you have completed your outlines, you will be fully prepared to start the actual writing.

The best way to approach outlining is with an open, flexible mind. Outlines can feel rigid, but they're not intended to trap or confine you–their purpose is to give you a big-picture view of your story; in that way, they can actually reduce your stress. Think of an outline as a roadmap; it's meant to guide you along a specific route, but that does not mean you are forbidden from taking side trips along the way. I like outlines because they help me test how far I can develop my ideas. If I outline an idea and see that I can take it really deep, then I know it's worth developing further. If I can't really flesh out an idea, then I know not to waste my time on it. Outlines can help prevent dead-ends in your plot as well as ensuring consistency in your writing.

The Elevator Pitch

I like to start out my outline by defining the storyline in one to three sentences. Pretend you're crafting an elevator pitch about your book. It should be short but packed with enough interesting details to stop people in their tracks.

First, describe your protagonist, either by name (if a well-known person) or by personality. Unless your protagonist is a household word, you should stick to generic terms in your storyline sentence. For example, if you had a protagonist named Stanley who was a loner, you would omit the name and just describe him as a loner. However, if your first book was a hit and you are now building a series upon it, by all means capitalize on the name recognition and thereby connect your readers to this new release.

Include:

- The situation at the start and your protagonist's goal

- The first plot twist or obstacle and the conflict that follows
- A mention of the antagonist

Here is an example of a storyline:

When a depressed loner (the protagonist) finally finds the woman of his dreams (the current situation), he vows to love her for life (the goal). But when this girl (the antagonist) falls for another man (the first plot twist or obstacle), the loner refuses to let go, stopping at nothing–not even revenge–to get her back (the conflict).

The Synopsis

After the summary, you will write your book's **synopsis.** A synopsis is a brief sketch of your storyline. You should always write your synopsis in the third person and using the present tense. Start with your plot outline, then expand upon it to create a story synopsis in a maximum of two pages. Touch on each plot twist and include major story events.

The first step in writing a synopsis is to flesh out the beginning of your story. Don't forget that this will be the first thing a prospective publisher will see. It also determines whether a reader will keep reading so skillfully insert your story hook and provide as much vivid action as possible. Highlight the first plot twist your protagonist encounters.

Next, summarize the middle of your story, highlighting the second and third plot twists. Toward the end of this section, you will summarize the events or issues that lead your characters toward their final confrontation.

Finally, sketch out the climax of the tale by describing its final conflict and showing briefly whether or not your protagonist achieves the desired objective. A solid synopsis will stand on its own, without needing further details. I encourage you to test your synopsis by asking someone who knows nothing about your story to read it and give you some feedback.

The Scene List

Another way to lay out your story is with a **scene list**. A scene list can provide a complete overview of your book in just a few pages, thus serving as a useful organizational tool. Scene lists make it easier to edit your book once you've finished. They assist you in identifying and deleting unnecessary scenes and can help you know exactly where is the best place to insert anything essential that has been overlooked.

To make a scene list, create a spreadsheet or a table with six columns. Label these columns "Scene Name," "Characters," "Point of View," "Location,"

"Summary," and "Moves Plot Forward?" then, starting with the first row, fill in the information for the first scene. In the first column, give your scene a name or other identifier. Moving to the right, list each character that appears in the scene, followed by whose point of view is used, and the location of the scene. Then write a couple of sentences briefly summarizing how the scene progresses and write "Yes" or "No," depending on whether or not the scene moves the plot forward. If it does not, then you may be able to omit the scene.

Each scene you write should be interrelated with the others and look to at least move toward answering the reader's questions and further development of the major themes of your book. For example, if you plan a scene in which your protagonist discovers he has a child he didn't know about, then you're going to need to set up the scene so your readers will say, "That makes sense." In this scenario, I would write an earlier scene where your protagonist and a respective character have a meeting where a secret could be revealed, but an argument breaks out and the secret is never told.

Some writers use flowcharts to portray the progression of their story. This involves using boxes to show movement from the exposition, to the rising action, on to the climax, and then to the resolution of your story. Boxes representing the development of themes usually run beneath the story flow.

Put aside some time to really focus on the ending of your book. Your ending will be your last contact with the reader; in it you have one final opportunity to leave a lasting impression. Break down your ending into several scenes that build suspense and lead to a strong and memorable resolution. Sometimes I am so strongly aware of how I want to end a book that I'll write the ending first; then I will work the story backwards from the ending. This reverse-order process enables me to space out the prerequisite details across previous scenes, giving various levels of obscure hints as to what is to come.

If later I find that the ending just doesn't work, I can always change it. Never think your work is wasted when you need to delete whole sections. Writing is a process, usually a process of trial and error. Every step you take is necessary, even if it looks like you are wasting whole chapters full of hard work. Each idea you scrap helps eliminate the unnecessary so that you can discover the best path for your story. Some books are like that. They will demand to go places you did not foresee. No worry; you can always rewrite as needed. If you're really strapped for ending ideas, take a few days off from writing. When you come back to it, first read through everything you have written, looking for leads you can pursue that might take you to a satisfying ending. Often, just backing away briefly will add enough objectivity to clarify where your story wants to take you.

Romance Cheat Sheet

As you recall, there are 5 key elements that make up a romance story:

1. An affectionate heroine
2. A charming and seductive hero
3. Emotional conflict
4. A realistic and engaging plot
5. A satisfying, happy ending

You can piece these elements together through the events you create. However, sometimes coming up with an outline, a synopsis and a scene list can be a challenge. I can help you here by describing the typical events that should happen in your romance story. Think of it as a formula to help you get started on your first romance story. After you have written a couple romances, the formula should come to you automatically and you will find it increasingly easy to move events around to fit your story:

The Meeting, otherwise usually known as the inciting incident, must happen at some point early on to get your story moving. Some authors like to introduce the hero and heroine to each other in the first chapter and others prefer to introduce each character separately. It's really up to you; however, just remember it has to happen early on. If your lovers meet halfway through the story, it won't work. Another point to note is that your hero and heroine do not have to fall in love right away. Instead, you should generate some sort of romantic connection, even if it only lasts for a few seconds. It can be anything that rivets their attention on each other.

After the initial meeting, your protagonist must either decide he or she is attracted to the love interest or deny the fact that there is an attraction.

The Lock Position is when a situation occurs that forces your hero and heroine to continue seeing each other. For example, if your two characters work together or walk their dogs in the same park every day, you've got yourself a lock position. The lock position provides a great opportunity to come up with conflict ideas. Think about what kind of lock position could create tension as well as romance.

Once you have developed the meeting and the lock position, you will then have to introduce the **Main Conflict** of the story. If your hero and heroine go on a date and immediately both decide they are meant for each other and have everything in common, you've got a terrible story on your hands. Introduce the conflicting goals of each character to create the main conflict. The conflict will serve as a symbol of what can keep the hero and heroine apart.

Next is **The Realization,** the point of no return, or the turning point. This is the moment when the hero and heroine are both emotionally invested in each other but the problems caused by the main conflict become significant. At this point in the story, the hero and heroine have no choice but to try and solve the problem. The protagonist usually thinks at this point, "I am in love" or "I can't get out of this situation." In this stage, you should portray the attraction between your characters as unique and irreplaceable.

After the realization is **The Breakup.** Some stories are structured so that the main conflict puts enough pressure on the hero and heroine to hit rock bottom, thus causing a breakup. In romance, a breakup is generated when the main conflict has not yet been resolved. Of course, you aren't required to include a breakup scene, but it does serve as a helpful plot point. Many readers have experienced breakups so this can certainly set the tone for a very emotional experience. If you do choose to include a breakup, make sure it is realistic but not over the top. Remember: your hero and heroine will have to get back together for the story to continue. If you've decided to include a breakup scene, the next scenes can be all about recovering emotionally, rediscovering the romance and getting back together. In this scene, your hero and heroine can approach one another, make up, and share a really memorable, romantic moment together.

The Resolution comes after the breakup and should lead to a happy outcome. At this point, the hero and heroine should solve the conflict and come back together. The conflict should be solved in a realistic manner – no cheating here. The ending should leave the reader feeling satisfied and inspired.

Help! I'm Stuck!

Finally, I love the outlining process because sometimes it helps me overcome writer's block. I'll be honest, if I have an idea, I'll often skip the outlining process and jump straight into sporadic writing and only return to the outline when I've encountered writer's block. As I said earlier, I believe the outlining process can be very inspiring and creative. With almost every story I've written, I've turned to outlining, at least eventually.

For example, writing a synopsis often helps me brainstorm ideas where the story goes to next. I might have my story written up the first plot point but then I'll be left clueless once I'm at the midpoint. At the first plot point, I can start asking myself, "Well what if..." and see if I can think of with a good midpoint scenario. I try to ask myself what my readers would and would not expect and pick the more exciting route (usually what they wouldn't expect). If I really cannot pick something, sometimes I'll invent a new character and find a way to work him or her in.

The outlining process also enables me to backtrack. If I'm writing a scene list and come across a scene that I think is boring, the outlining process allows me to go back and rework it rather than just scrapping it altogether. It also enables me to take a break from writing one scene and jump to another if I can't figure out where to take it.

Some other things you can do to help beat writers' block are to do some research for inspiration or experiment with switching point of view. Research sounds awful but sometimes it can be really fun! For example, I thought about writing a story about gangs, but I have no knowledge of gangs or how they work, so I read a memoir about gangs to get a better idea. Switching the point of view in a scene is more like a creative writing activity to help you gain a more rounded view of your story and characters.

Finally, I've always found that simply taking a break helps me. Sitting at a computer for long hours can be draining. I know that I usually get tired and hungry, so I'll go grab a bite to eat, do something fun for a little bit (maybe listen to music or watch a show), just get my eyes away from the screen and I'll usually come back feeling refreshed. I also always go back over the parts of the story I wrote as my tiredness was setting in because eight out of ten times I find that's where I start rushing and slacking off.

Chapter 6: Romance Writing - Tips and Strategies

Write Stunning Love Scenes

Love scenes reside in the heart of most romance novels. Have you ever read a love scene that was so well written you found yourself fully engaged, both mentally and physically, feeling as if you were part of the action? Mastering this skill can help you connect emotionally with your readers and may just give your romance stories the push they need to become successful in the marketplace.

First, you'll want to determine the kind of love scene you're comfortable reading and writing. Although erotica has risen in popularity lately, this doesn't necessarily mean you have to write steamy love scenes to become successful. There are as many readers who enjoy a subtle, sensual love scene as who enjoy immersing themselves in graphic erotica. If you're not comfortable depicting raw sexual encounters, don't force yourself to this extreme; if you do, your writing may feel stilted and forced. Most importantly, don't cop out on your readers. They buy romance novels because they want, precisely, romance. Don't take them on an emotional ride, set them up, and then fail to include a romantic highlight in your book. Remember, a romantic climax doesn't have to be erotic, but you should include at least *some* sort of love scene in your book. Otherwise, you'll have trouble convincing people that you have written a romance novel!

Next, be as realistic as possible. Avoid making your love scenes boring to the point that readers will skip beyond them, but also shy away from excessive emotionalism. As long as you've paid close attention to developing your characters, your love scenes should almost automatically read true to life. Experiment while writing love scenes to see how you can work in the flaws of your hero and heroine; this will add the conflict and tension that only increases a scene's pulling power. Do not entirely omit the physical attraction that must exist between your hero and heroine. Your readers *want* to experience this. In fact, you should portray the attraction between your main characters as early as possible, weaving subtle hints into their thoughts and body language. Of course, these hints of physical and emotional attraction should grow in detail throughout your book until the full reveal of the love scene becomes a long-awaited next step. Don't be afraid to integrate the five senses into your love scenes so that readers will receive everything they've been anticipating for all these many pages.

The key is really to balance the physical and mental aspects of your love scene. Your readers want to experience both a physical and an emotional change. An over-emphasis on physical details with too little emotional input – or vice versa – can cause a reader to put your book down faster than you can say "romance." A good way to test your writing balance is to ask yourself if you're just writing love scenes to fill pages. Filler love scenes can lose their emotional appeal quickly and have been known to drive readers away in droves. By contrast, your best and most effective love scenes will help move the plot forward. Look for ways to reveal something new about your character. Use the tension this engenders to bump up your characters' emotions or otherwise carry your readers with you toward the end of your story.

Once you've figured out these parts of your love scenes, the next step is to write the dialogue, if you haven't started already. A silent love scene is boring. You want it to appear as alive as possible. Your dialogue doesn't have to be elaborate; it only needs to contribute enough tension to reveal to your readers the sensual attraction as it grows throughout the scene. In general, dialogue in a love scene is usually serious but if the atmosphere allows, go ahead and insert some comedy as a temporary relief before the attraction develops to the next level.

Finally, read your love scene out loud to see if it stands the ultimate test. If the passage gets your emotions blazing, then you're probably good to go. If it does not generate any response, if it doesn't sound right, or if it triggers the wrong emotion – such as laughter – you should probably go back and make some changes. Keep reading your scene out loud until you've achieved the emotion you want your readers to feel.

Add Some Danger

What's more exciting and attention-grabbing than a little bit of danger and romance mixed together? If you feel your storyline dragging, see if you can add in an element of danger. It doesn't have to be anything too crazy. It can be as simple as a bad car accident that sets the scene for the hero to swoop in and save the day. A little bit of danger can wake up your audience and hold their attention.

To Subplot … or Not

Skip the subplots if you're not trying to write an epic romance. In-depth romance novels often include interesting subplots, but if you're trying to bang out some short stories to post on Kindle, it's best to focus on the center storyline. If you do decide to write a bigger novel and want to include subplots, save them for the revision phase; that way you won't be distracted from writing a solid central storyline.

I think the best way to create a subplot is to write it out as its own standalone short story and then edit into your main plot, usually introducing it near to the end. This way, you won't forget any important details in the main story and you won't accidentally detract from the punch of the central storyline. If you're looking to add some elements of danger into your story, a subplot can be a good idea.

Create Straightforward Characters

Human relationships are complex and often confusing. You, or one of your friends, may have felt their significant other was "playing games" or otherwise not being honest and straightforward. Your readers lose themselves in a romance in order to escape from real life and the everyday challenges of their existing relationships. Therefore, while you should make your characters *realistic*, don't make them *too* realistic. In other words, your readers want to escape, so don't serve up a carbon copy of their life.

When Unsure, Use Sex or Humor

Not sure where to take your story next? Throw in a sex scene (ensuring that it fits the context of your story, of course) or add in some humor. Although romance readers tend to prefer their stories on the serious side, a little lighthearted refreshment never turned anyone away. Plus, it can add to the development of your characters.

Naming Your Romance

The title of your romance story is vital to attracting readers. You want to say it all to the reader who is browsing the shelves looking for a fresh book. Your title should give your potential audience a glimpse of what the story is about. It is likely the first thing they will see, so it is important to create the most compelling title possible. Remember, you only have a few seconds to convince a person to choose your book over the myriad romances that crowd the shelf, so any time spent developing a knockout title will be worth much more than what it costs you in time.

It is not uncommon for a romance story to include the word "Love" in the title. Find an additional word or two that best represent the premise of your story. For example, a story about a love triangle might be called "One Love." A romance between a police officer and his lover could be entitled "Charged with Love." Grab a dictionary or thesaurus and see what you can come up with that speaks to your story premise.

Another option is to integrate the career of your hero or heroine into the title. For example, "Gambler's Paradise" or "Painting Love." You can also include the name of the love interest in the title. This tactic is best paired with alliteration. "Marrying Michael" or "Chasing Chastity," are examples of the use of alliteration, coupled with characters' names.

A fun way to create a perfect title is to brainstorm. First, make a list of emotions that are related to romance, such as "passion" and "tension." Then list potential situations, such as "vengeance" or "denial." Next, create a list of romance-related actions like "love, claim, kiss, or hold." Then create a list of pronouns. Put each word on a small piece of paper and mix them up in a bag. Pull out a handful of words and see if you can string them together to create an enticing title. For example, you might pick out words that create "Passionate Vengeance" or

"Wanting Her." Experiment with multiple combinations of words, mixing and matching phrases to generate several potentially impactful titles.

Find a Happy Starting Point

In romance, it is important to not start too soon, but not start too late, either. Starting out too soon usually means opening up with a backstory. Starting out too late usually entails diving right into the story without letting your readers get to know the main characters. Both extremes short-circuit the reader's ability to immerse themselves in your story. Give them time to get to know the hero and heroine. I personally like to reveal aspects of a character's backstory throughout the novel. If you're writing a short story or a novella, this may be a little more challenging, but you can use the "show don't tell" rule to help your readers get to know your main characters.

Choose Descriptive Words Carefully

Nearly every word in a romance story can deliver a zap of emotion to your readers. Therefore, it is important to carefully pick your descriptive words. One word can make all the difference in a scene. The best way to pick the most appropriate words is to make them match the mood of the scene. For example, the words "ran" and "jolted" have the same basic meaning – to move forward quickly – but depending on the context of the scene they're used in, they can have a staggering difference in emotional intensity. If the mood of your scene is lighthearted and warm, using the word "ran" may fit in well. However, if the mood of your scene is urgent and dangerous, "jolted" may be a better fit. Let's use the two in an example:

"Brittany ran from the train platform into Michael's arms." When you read a sentence like this, you're probably envisioning a scene where the heroine lays eyes on her fiancé for the first time in weeks, and then races eagerly into his open arms for the long awaited reunion

"Brittany jolted from the train platform into Michael's arms." In this sentence, the word jolted provides an additional sense of urgency. Readers might envision the heroine running from danger into her fiancé's arms; it allows the hero's protective instincts to surface and can be used to take a relationship to the next level of intensity.

Use Literary Devices

Similes, metaphors, and analogies can really spice up a scene by helping your readers paint a vivid picture of each scene. Tie each of these devices to an emotion such as happiness, anger, or surprise, in order to allow your characters' personalities to pop out into multiple dimensions. For example, the sentence, "Her perfume smelled like a fresh ocean breeze," can pull the smell of perfume right off the page. Saying, "He was as angry as a disturbed swarm of bees" can immerse your reader in all the agitation of the character's wrath.

Chapter 7: Romantic Storylines

Hopefully, by the time you've reached this chapter, you've started to picture your own romance story playing out in your head. Or, maybe not. Romance is a broad genre with many stories being cranked out every day, so it can be hard to come up with original ideas. Though a successful romance book largely depends on your characters, not the idea itself, it is true that a single idea can help you get the ball rolling. Most romance storylines are unoriginal and widely used. In this chapter, you will discover some of the most popular ones that can help you start piecing ideas together.

Get Creative

If there is one thing to beware of in romance writing, it is this: practically every idea has been used before. The task of coming up with an original romance is definitely possible, but it can also be very challenging, especially if you begin to suspect your storyline is beginning to sound like a familiar movie, TV show or book. The easiest way to develop an original romance idea is to start out with a basic cliché and then take it from there. For example, you could start out with "the guy next door" or "the secretary affair." Don't panic when you hear the word "cliché." Here's the good news: *romance fans love them*. Another benefit of using clichés is that they come with built-in conflict structures.

What really makes your romance story original is your characters. As in real life, different personalities react differently in any given situation. A newly married husband will react to a cheating wife differently than will an older man who has been married for forty years. A hero who drinks too much will have a different response to his relationship responsibilities than a hero who is completely sober. And hey, who said your characters have to be humans? Paranormal romance is a huge subgenre, with a substantial highly devoted reading audience.

Where Do Your Characters Meet?

Your hero and heroine can meet anywhere. You can choose a random, nondescript place or a location that ties into to the deep backstory of a character or otherwise speaks to the details of setting. Here are some common places that couples meet in real life:

- Bars, parties, BBQs or other social events with mutual friends
- The beach
- During a fun activity (laser tags, arcades, go karts, etc.)
- Winery, brewery, museum or other kind of tour

- A convention or festival
- A sporting event or concert
- In nature (hiking, mountain climbing.)
- On a blind date set up by friends
- At a college
- Through a public service (e.g., nurse who treats a patient)
- Accidental run-in (e.g., they bump into each other at the library)
- Online dating

What Keeps Your Characters Stuck in the Same Vicinity?

- Job assignments
- Neighbors or roommates
- Stranded together (e.g., stuck in the airport or in an elevator)
- Mutual friends
- Connected to hero or heroine's children
- In the same class
- Participation in the same interests

Opposites Attract

This theme is popular because it reflects a common societal assumption. This theme appears when the hero and heroine clash initially, but get stuck together in some sort of situation. After the hero and heroine establish their dislike for each other, there is usually a revelation or an event that changes their attitude toward the other person. For example, a hero might rescue the heroine from a dangerous situation, causing her to look at him in a positive way.

Hidden Identity

Hidden identity themes are great for writing suspenseful and exciting romance stories. In this type of story, the hero or heroine usually harbors a secret, such as pretending to be someone else to cover up a sordid past. Everything seems perfect and the two start to like each other. When the hidden identity is revealed you have instant tension and the characters face a major challenge. The deceptive character eventually explains the motive behind the disguise, usually providing a reasonable explanation. Eventually, everything settles down until the next plot twist stirs the pot again.

Single Parents

Single parent romance stories focus on the hero or heroine raising a child alone. Given the high percentage of single-parent households today, this is a theme that may only grow in popularity. Oftentimes, the love interest will be introduced through the child, where it surfaces as the parent meets a coach, a teacher or a parent of the child's friend. Single parent romance stories can fit any subgenre and are often lighthearted. In the end, the hero and heroine commit to each other and we assume they live happily ever after.

Woman Needing Rescue

The "woman needing rescue" theme is a classic romance story idea. Usually the needy woman becomes the love interest after the hero sets out to save her. As he rescues her, they both form a connection and it becomes the hero's job to protect the heroine throughout the story. Sometimes the hero's goal is to rescue the heroine for a third party but ends up falling in love with her himself.

More than Just Friends

Some romance stories begin with two friends who end up romantically involved. Often, the hero or the heroine will have an existing love interest at the beginning of the book but will, in the person of another character, discover their soul mate. The main challenge for the characters in this type of story is the process of finding the strength to let go of the original partner.

Pretend Lovers

Romance stories about pretend lovers make exciting and engaging stories. These tales usually begin with a hero or heroine for hire. Sometimes the main character will ask the love interest to pretend to be an existing partner, either to prove something to others or to keep other pursuers away. Although the relationship starts out as fake, the hero or heroine usually captures the interest of the partner and they both end up falling in love.

Bad Boy/Girl Turns Good

Many readers love romance stories that focus on a bad boy (or a girl) who changes into a better person. In most cases, the hero is the rebellious one until he meets the heroine, who eventually inspires him to change for the better. The bad boy is often involved in a dangerous situation, such as a gang, the mafia or importing illegal goods. By the end of the story, the hero is no longer involved in the dangerous lifestyle and is ready to settle into a stable relationship.

Return Home (Reunion)

Another great idea for a romance story is to have the hero and heroine previously know each other and then reunite. An event often occurs to bring the hero and heroine together, usually a funeral, a high school reunion or a get-together with old friends. The hero and heroine, who haven't seen each other in years, start talking and eventually develop feelings for each other. Sometimes the hero or heroine is attracted to an old friend in the beginning, but meets and falls in love with a new friend.

Chasing Wrong Love

Chasing after the wrong love is a popular theme in romance. Usually, the hero or heroine starts off engaged to somebody, then meets a new love interest and starts to question the original relationship. The questioning is often dragged out and delayed until the last minute. One example is a hero who crashes the heroine's wedding in order to confess his true feelings. Another common scenario is the heroine who backs out of her original relationship the night before the nuptials take place.

Widows

Romance stories featuring widows usually focus on heroes or heroines who are recently widowed and find themselves re-entering the dating scene. This type of story gives writers a great deal of room to think creatively and give the story some unique twists and turns.

Beauty and the Beast

Beauty and the beast stories are classic love stories about a beautiful heroine falling in love with a hero who is less attractive and sometimes monstrous. Despite the hero's looks, the heroine must find something in the hero's character that is solid enough to support falling in love. The theme here is that looks aren't everything.

Social Class Differences

Romance featuring social class differences makes for great stories full of cross-cultural conflict and tension. The hero and heroine are strongly attracted to each other but are challenged by the implications of differences in their backgrounds. Frequently, the families of both main characters get involved, only complicating the plot.

Competitors who Fall in Love

Competitors who fall in love can lead the reader on a delightful and action-packed romp. These stories often revolve around sports figures, but can include the arts, medicine, or the corporate boardroom. Sometimes the hero and heroine play on different teams, eventually communicating with each other and starting to fall in love. The challenge here rests in the competition, professional and personal, between the two characters.

Long Distance Relationships

Stories about long distance relationships are another popular idea for writing romances. The hero and heroine start out in an existing relationship with each other, or they meet and are separated soon thereafter. Common settings are the military, a job transfer after the initial meeting, and the sometimes clichéd meeting while on vacation. The challenge in a long distance relationship consists of the hero and heroine not being able to physically see each other every day. This could raise the stakes for cheating and infidelity, making love triangles a possibility.

Chapter 8: The Grand Finale

Writing the ending of your romance story is a unique experience. When you are writing any other genre of fiction, you can go either way with the ending: you can make it happy or sad. However, the thing about romance is that your readers automatically expect a happy ending, leaving you very little wiggle room for a shocker, unless you plan on a cliffhanger. Critics of romance argue that romantic endings are unrealistic and disappointing because real life doesn't always work out that way, but the happy ending is one reason romance is such a popular genre. It feeds into our natural desire for everything to work out in the end.

The good news is that if you're an author who loves to add a shock factor to your stories, you can still do this. The only major change is in location; you will need to insert the shocker nearer to the middle of your tale. Your readers *want* the hero and heroine to come together at the end but you can play with their emotions by having the hero and heroine split up or be on the verge of splitting up somewhere earlier in the story. Not only *can* you add this shock factor to your book but you *should*. It can be vital in keeping your readers hooked.

Some writers feel challenged by the requirement for a super sweet ending. This can be especially true for writers who have never experienced a real-life romance for themselves. If you are an author in this position, you actually have an advantage, because you can write out of your own desire. Once you've written an ending you would love to experience in real life, you can be fairly confident your readers will feel satisfied, as well. Remember: the most satisfying endings usually close with a kiss.

An optional technique you can use to solidify your ending is to tie in the theme. You can simply repeat what you wrote in your narrative summary. You can even come right out and state your theme in what may feel like the corniest way ever. Stating the theme at the end of your romance serves a second purpose: it can help your readers feel like the story has been wrapped up nicely with a bow. For example, if the theme of your story is "good things come to those who wait," you could end with a sentence like, "Lauren's grandmother was indeed right; good things *do* come to those who wait." As cheesy as it may sound, the cheesiness will go right over your readers' heads and they will revel in the affirmation of their beliefs.

Writing the perfect ending to your romance story is important, because the ending can determine whether readers will buy another book penned by you.

On Writing Cliffhangers

Cliffhangers are useful in priming your readers to want more and ensuring a ready-made audience for the next installment in your book series. Your reading public will want to know what happens next, although it can be frustrating for them to have to wait until the next volume is released. A well-written cliffhanger at the end of an amazing romance story can leave readers talking about it up until the next installment comes out! Here's how to write an amazing cliffhanger:

Obviously, save the cliffhanger for the end of your book. Your reader will have nowhere else to go after expecting a conclusion, so this is good way to insert some delicious shock factor. Sometimes authors provide small cliffhangers at the end of previous chapters, but they will save the best cliffhanger, the one that makes readers go crazy, for last. If you do include a cliffhanger, make it quick and sudden. Don't allow your readers to see it coming. Then, in the next installment, immediately address the cliffhanger. Remember, your readers have been waiting a long time to have their questions answered. If you don't provide answers right away, you risk losing their interest and their readership for other books you release in the future.

Not sure how to write a cliffhanger? Here are several strategies you can try. First, re-read some examples of cliffhangers in your favorite books and try to see how the author set them up. Then try to think of a cliffhanger that you would like to read in your book. Since you'll probably already know how your cliffhanger will play out, ask a friend or family member to read your final chapter and see how well the cliffhanger works for them.

A Final Note on Endings

You can always write your ending first. This is usually how I write. If I have a strong idea, I tend to know how I want the story to end, so I write my ending first to capture my ideas in their rawest state. I always find that writing the ending first enables me to better set up my story as I write through it. However, sometimes I'm not sure how I want the story to end. In that case, I will start writing and trust that the ending will make itself known later. If you write your ending first, remember that you can always go back and change it as needed. Nothing is ever set in concrete until your book is in print.

Conclusion

I hope this book was able to help you to discover how to successfully write a romance story that has the potential to be a best seller. The most important truths to remember are that most storylines are unoriginal, so it's really your characters who will dictate the success of your book. Romance writing requires a great deal of creativity and open-minded thinking, but it *is* possible to develop an original idea and become the next top author!

Your next step is to start thinking about your story, its characters, and some major plot twists. These three items will make up the bulk of your book. Be sure to start out by preparing yourself to write a book in the best way possible. Light up some candles, put on some relaxing music and let your imagination run free. Once you've gotten ready, start outlining your story basics: the plot, the setting, and all the other elements we talked about in Chapter Two. Afterwards, dedicate the majority of your time to developing your characters. They will lead you toward success. Remember to develop the personality and physical appearance of the protagonist and the love interest in as much detail as possible. Then, start thinking about your characters' story goals and the basics of your storyline; this will keep your readers hooked from beginning to end.

Once you have all those ideas straightened out, you can start to outline your story. Although you don't have to have an outline, I highly recommend it for staying organized and becoming successful. Finally, spend a healthy amount of time writing the ending. Don't forget that your readers want it to be a happy one! Then, wrap up everything you've worked on and get ready to show off your story to the world!

My Other Books and Audio Books

All of these are available in audio book as well.

If you enjoyed this book then please spare a few seconds to easily post a quick positive review. It would be greatly appreciated!

Thanks for reading.

www.ingramcontent.com/pod-product-compliance
Lightning Source LLC
Chambersburg PA
CBHW051422070526
44584CB00023B/3547